AMERICA IN THE WAR

III

HOW WE WENT TO WAR

Ships building at Hog Island.

"More vessels will leave the ways in one year than all the English yards have ever been able to build in the same time."

[*Page* 39]

AMERICA IN THE WAR

HOW WE WENT TO WAR

BY

NELSON LLOYD

ILLUSTRATED

NEW YORK
CHARLES SCRIBNER'S SONS
1918

CONTENTS

ILLUSTRATIONS

HOW WE WENT TO WAR

CHAPTER I

INTRODUCTION

THERE is nothing finer in American history than the way in which the American people, as a whole, responded to the call for war with Germany. This statement might seem too broad. Some critics might take issue with it. They might point to the peace-at-any-price campaign which was wide-spread over the country from the beginning of the World War in 1914 to the very hour when America was forced to take up arms. They might point to sporadic outbursts of disloyalty by certain foreign-born elements of our population, who placed the cause of the lands of their birth above the welfare of their adopted country. They might point to certain members of Congress, even, who by their obstructionist tactics gave evidence of lukewarmness for the war, and even of outright lack of patriotism. Every community has

had its pacifists, its pacifists with honest hearts
and weak heads, its dishonest pacifists working
in the interest of the country's enemy, its slackers, its malcontents. This has been true of
every nation in every past war. But certain it
is that when on April 6, 1917, our government
accepted the German challenge to our rights
and liberties, the American people ranged themselves behind their leaders with a steadfast purpose to meet their heavy task, to make every
sacrifice that the world might be freed from
the horror of German militarism and Kultur.

Look at their record.

In the first eighteen months of the war by the
volunteer system and the selective draft they
raised their armies from hardly 250,000 men to
3,000,000, of whom more than one-half were
moved to the battle-front in France.

Their navy was increased by volunteers from
65,000 men to over 500,000, and ships by the
hundred were added to their sea force.

Starting with an almost negligible number of
merchant vessels, they had laid the foundation
of the greatest merchant marine in the world.

During the same period they had paid to

their government more than $4,000,000,000 in taxes, and had advanced to it in loans by the purchase of Liberty Bonds and War Savings Stamps more than $9,000,000,000.

To make easier the lives of their fighting men and to heal the wounds inflicted on the world by German Kultur, they had given, through the Red Cross, the Y. M. C. A., the Knights of Columbus, and other philanthropic agencies, full a half-billion dollars. But, above all, they had offered the lives of their men and their women and stood ready to bear increasing sorrows and heavier burdens.

These figures are not to be read in a spirit of boastfulness. America has not yet had to drain the very dregs of the cup of sorrow, as have France and Great Britain, Belgium, Serbia, and Italy. America has not had to stand with her back to the wall to meet the onslaught of hordes of modern savages, the product of years of a system of perverted education, based on a perverted system of morality. These figures are given because they answer the charges of the Germans abroad and the Germans at home, that the American people were not wholeheartedly in the war. They answer the old argument of the pacifists that the American people would not suffer themselves to be dragged into a conflict 3,000 miles away, and would endure dishonor and outrage rather than fight in defense of their own and the world's liberty. The things that the Germans and pacifists said the Americans would not do they have done, and they have done it in full measure.

It is true that following the outbreak of the European War we had two and a half years of divided opinion and hesitation, but those were years of education and they brought us to a common opinion and a common purpose. Had the heads of our government been less idealistic, of less pacific minds, that period might have been briefer and we might have faced the conflict better prepared for it. They did not lead the people to war. They did not even teach the people to prepare for war. Their every effort was to keep the country at peace. But they, too, were learning. Few people in the United States at the beginning of the World War realized the peril that lay in Germany's aggression. Few had ever heard of the Pan-

German movement. Few believed that Germany was really carrying out a well-laid scheme to secure the rule of the world by force. The full depth of Germany's guilt was not known. When the neutrality of Belgium was violated and there followed a series of excesses that shocked civilization, some public men and writers did proclaim our danger and warn us to make ready to meet it. But the lesson was learned slowly. The rape of Belgium shocked all decent people, but Belgium was three thousand miles away, and we did not see those horrors close at hand. It took time to reveal them to us. Military necessity was the excuse of Germany's apologists, and with some it found credence. We did not realize that the Belgium horror was but a part of a long-laid plan to bring the world to its knees under the lash of frightfulness. That a nation supposed to be civilized could commit such crimes seemed incredible.

In 1915 blinking eyes began to open wide. Clouds of poison-gas were rolled across the British front, dealing a hideous death to gallant soldiers who were fighting fairly, and Germany was seen again violating the rules of warfare laid down by The Hague conventions to which she had acceded. While men still had faith in her honor, her scientists were experimenting on cats and dogs to devise the cruellest form of weapon for her army's use. Liquid fire followed the gas, and then began the murderous career of her submarines.

From the first the sympathy of the great majority of Americans was with the Allies. Even then Germany might have taught us to respect her. She taught us to despise. Her declaration of a war zone around her enemies' coasts on February 4, 1915, gave us the first real warning of trouble ahead. The right of American ships and American citizens to traverse the seas in time of war was firmly established by long-standing principles of international law. If Germany could have maintained a blockade of enemy ports the case would have been different, but even then she would have had to safeguard the lives of passengers and crews of both enemy and neutral merchant vessels. This she could not do. Her navy, except her submarines, had been driven from the seas, and, disregarding President Wilson's warning that she would be held to "strict accountability" for her acts, she sent those submarines forth on their mission of piracy. On March 28 the British steamship *Falaba* was sent to the bottom with 111 lives; on April 8 the *Harpalyce*, carrying food to starving Belgium, was torpedoed, and fifteen of the crew were lost. Vessel after vessel was sunk without warning. It was the sinking of the Cunard liner *Lusitania* on May 7 that fanned America's anger into full flame. By that crowning murder 1,154 men, women, and children lost their lives, and of these 114 were Americans. This alone was enough to convince the unbiassed of the sinister nature of Germany's plans and the peril to the world in the victory of such a people.

Had the German Government deliberately planned to open the eyes of America to Germany's intentions and to the danger that lay behind those intentions, it could not have acted more efficiently. Slowly the whole system of frightfulness was unfolded, and the perversion of the German mind laid bare. Despite our warnings, ship after ship was murderously sunk.

German Zeppelins and airplanes dropped their bombs on open towns, dealing death to hundreds of innocent men, women, and children. There was no respect for that emblem of mercy, the Red Cross. The wounded and the nurses of the hospitals became fair game for any Hunnish warrior of the air, and hospital-ships, with their freight of wounded, choice marks for those that lurked under the sea. Even as I write comes the news of the sinking of the hospital-ship *Llandovery Castle*, when on an errand of mercy, and 258 persons, including 14 women nurses, were killed.

Future historians, reviewing the events of these times, will certainly wonder at those two and a half years when America endured so many wrongs at Germany's hands, and took no other action than to strive to bring her to reason by argument, unsupported by even a show of force. They will wonder why, when the threat was so evident, we made no preparation to meet the storm. The truth is we had a pacific and altruistically minded administration; we had a Congress which contained a large number of pacifists, some pacifists from sin-

cerely patriotic motives, and others for reasons purely selfish. To-day no man in the
world is more hated by the Germans than
President Wilson. They charge him with being
a tool of Great Britain, and with deliberately
leading us to war, to the ruin of their hope for
victory and world dominion. Nothing could be
more false. He strove patiently to keep us at
peace, often in the face of bitter opposition at
home, but that day came, when, as he has said:
"The right is more precious than peace." From
that day he has been for "force, force to the
utmost," and he has had behind him a united
Congress and a united people. But they were
not for war because, as a German has written,
"war is the most august of all human activities"; they were for war because only by war
could the world be made "a decent place in
which to live."

"The object of America in this war," the
President has said, "is to deliver the free peoples of the world from the menace and the
actual power of a vast military establishment,
controlled by an irresponsible government,
which, having secretly planned to dominate the

world, proceeded to carry out the plan without regard either to the sacred obligations of treaty or the long-established practices and long-cherished principles of international action and honor; which chose its own time for the war, delivered its blow fiercely and suddenly, stopped at no barrier, either of law or mercy, swept a whole continent within the tide of blood—not the blood of soldiers only, but the blood of innocent women and children, also, and of the helpless poor, and now stands, balked but not defeated, the enemy of four-fifths of the world. . . ."

We can imagine the historian puzzling over the question as to why we were so long in discovering this menace, why we did not see it when Belgium was overrun and ruined, and the *Lusitania* sunk. His perspective will be better than ours. He will be able to trace the whole series of great events from their beginning to their end. He will find the germs of the war in those days fifty years ago when the Germans overran France and formed the German Empire, with Prussia at its head. He will review Germany's fifty years of military preparation. He

will study the outpourings of Germany's statesmen, her educators, her publicists, and see them
all tending to instil in the German mind a desire for conquest, and to prepare the people for
a sudden rush that would carry them on the
first stage toward world domination. He will
marvel that the rest of the world was so blind
as not to foresee what lay ahead and prepare
for it.

There were, before the war, in France and
England some far-sighted men who urged their
people to make ready for a German attack, but
it is doubtful if even these realized the com-
pleteness of Germany's preparations or her contemplated barbarity of warfare. It was incredible that a great modern nation should have been
drilled and educated into a race of barbarians.

Lord Roberts warned England, and England,
lost in a maze of party squabbles and Irish
quarrels, did not listen, so that when the German hordes struck into France she could only
send against them an army of 150,000 men. A
gallanter army never went to battle, but it was
hopelessly outnumbered and almost wiped out.
For our own lack of preparation before 1914

there was good reason. We were separated from Europe by 3,000 miles of sea, and it did not seem that we could ever be involved in a European conflict or threatened seriously by a European Power. For our policy of unpreparedness after 1914 there was less reason, for we had before us a lesson to study—the events in Belgium and France, and incident after incident which betrayed the German method and true purpose. We had our public men who foresaw our danger, and warned us, even if we did not go to war, to prepare for eventualities. We did not listen. We did order a considerable increase in our naval establishment, but as to our army we did practically nothing.

It is a fact that at the beginning of the war we had many pronounced pacifists in places of influence in the government. Our foreign relations were in the hands of William J. Bryan, whose hobby was peace maintained by treaty and arbitration, an excellent, but at that time an unworkable, plan. When war threatened us he was for peace at almost any price and against military preparation. His declaration that a million Americans would spring to arms overnight if danger threatened us has become a hackneyed joke. However, he did sign those two able notes which President Wilson sent to Germany on the sinking of the *Lusitania*, and then, finding the American people becoming warlike and out of sympathy with his policies, retired. He was followed by Robert Lansing, who has conducted the State Department with dignity and courage, and in the spirit of its best traditions.

The then Secretary of War, Lindley M. Garrison, seeing trouble ahead, did make every effort to secure some measure of military preparation, but he met opposition in both houses of Congress, and he did not seem to have hearty support from most of the other members of the administration. There was a theory that to arm thoroughly would be a threat to Germany which might disarrange the delicate negotiations then proceeding. Besides, Count von Bernstorff and his army of propagandists were active in holding us to the ways of peace. Universal service on a modified scale was talked of, but the politicians declared that the American peo-

ple would never suffer such a system. Mr.
Garrison tried to obtain a compromise with his
plan for a "continental army," an army of
500,000 volunteers serving part time, but this,
too, was blocked, and on June 3, 1916, the National Defense Act was passed which made the
inadequately trained National Guards of the
States into a second line of national military
defense. Under this act the government was
authorized to recruit the Guard up to 300,000
men, while the war strength authorized for the
regular army was raised to 287,000. Mr. Garrison retired and was succeeded by Newton D.
Baker, who had been mayor of Cleveland, a
man generally credited at that time with holding pronounced pacifist principles. Certainly
under Mr. Baker's leadership in the months
preceding our entry into the war little was done
to strengthen our military arm in any large
way. There began a wide-spread agitation for
preparedness all over the country. Mass-meet-
ings were held; great parades, emphasizing the
demand, marched the streets; many patriotic
organizations carried on a campaign of education, but little effective work was done by the

government. There could be only two reasons
for this. The first is political. The men of all
parties, who had the power to act effectively,
misread the character of the mass of the American people and feared for their political future.
The second is ignorance and lack of foresight.
Having little knowledge of German history and
German character, they sincerely believed that
we were able to continue honorably at peace.
The President himself, a year before the war
broke out, declared in a public speech that we
were in no danger from any quarter. Some
time later he weakened and declared that this
was the last great war America could keep out
of. One conspicuous man who did see the
danger, warned us of it, and acted to the best of
his limited power, was General Leonard Wood.
By establishing a series of camps for intensive
military training he secured the nucleus of the
great corps of officers we were so soon to need.

Meanwhile the eyes of the Americans, from
the President down, were being opened to the
true menace of Germany. Mr. Wilson worked
patiently to bring Germany to reason and to
avoid war honorably, but he and the whole

people were fast losing patience. Those who
failed to see in Germany's atrocities in Europe
and on the seas, or in her violations of international law, a just reason for our entering the
war, were aroused when she was caught carrying on in our own neutral land a campaign of
violence and intrigue. Factories were blown
up, infernal machines were placed on our merchantmen, strikes were fomented, efforts were
made to destroy our rail and water communica-
tions. Two attachés of the embassy, Captains
Boy-Ed and Von Papen, were caught and sent
home. Still we were patient and the arch-
plotter, Count von Bernstorff, remained. The
Germans fooled themselves. It was a common
argument of theirs that the Americans were a
people sunk in the sloth of prosperity, who
thought of nothing but the dollar, and were
deaf to the calls of honor and justice. Could
they clean up Europe, the German supermen
would make short work of these imbeciles.
They misread President Wilson—a college pro-
fessor, they said, given to words, not action,
especially warlike action. Brazenly they broke
all their promises, and tore up all their agree-

ments with us. It was on January 31, 1917, that their government announced that it would sink without warning the vessels of any nationality found in certain areas of the seas surrounding their enemies. The one thing to do, the President did promptly. On February 3 he broke off diplomatic relations with Germany.

The breaking of diplomatic relations between states does not of necessity lead to war. In this case, considering the temper of the German mind, war seemed inevitable, and yet we made no great effort to be ready for it. The navy was tuned up, and work was rushed on the new vessels on the ways, but save for a flurry of recruiting for the army and the National Guard, to bring them up to their full peace strength, our military forces were not augmented. For two months more we endured with fair equanimity German intrigue, outrage, and insult. Ship after ship was sunk without warning, with the loss of many lives. Not content with this, Germany was endeavoring to stir Japan and Mexico to war with us, as was discovered by the intercepting of a note of January 19 from the German Foreign Office to the German minister in Mexico. There was nothing left but war. President Wilson met the issue, and Congress and the people stood ready to support him to the utmost.

"The right is more precious than peace," said the President in his address to Congress on April 2, "and we shall fight for the things which we have always carried nearest our hearts— for democracy, for the right of those who submit to authority to have a voice in their own governments, for the rights and liberties of small nations, for a universal dominion of right by such a concert of free people as shall bring peace and safety to all nations and make the world itself at last free.

"To such a task we can dedicate our lives and our fortunes, everything that we are and everything that we have with the pride of those who know that the day has come when America is privileged to spend her blood and her might for the principles that gave her birth and happiness and the peace which she has treasured.

"God helping her, she can do no other."

America could, indeed, do no other. She girded herself for the task.

CHAPTER II

THE TASK

SUCH a task! To accomplish it demanded the co-ordination of all the energies and all the industries in the country. Our enemy was 3,000 miles away, over a sea infested by his merciless submarines. He had overrun nearly all of Belgium and a goodly part of northern France, and stood intrenched from the English Channel to the Swiss border; he had conquered Serbia, Montenegro, and half of Rumania. In the east Russia still held, but only feebly. On March 3 the Czar had abdicated, and when we became Russia's ally she was in control of a government too unstable to be relied on, however good its intentions. Russia's military assistance had become even then almost nil. Our allies, France, Great Britain, and Italy, were worn by more than two years of the cruellest war in history. To us they looked for food to fill their depleted larders, for raw materials and fuel for their munition factories, for finished munitions for their armies, and for soldiers to fight with those armies and help them drive the Germans over the Rhine. To transport the food, materials, and men, the sea had to be made safe and ships found. The food had to be raised, the fuel and metals mined, the armies drilled and equipped.

Fortunately, we came to the task a united people, more than 100,000,000 strong, possessing the richest country in the world. It has been argued in some quarters that had our government not shown such patience in its intricate dealings with Germany, but had brought us earlier into the conflict, it would have found a people less united on war, and in their purpose to carry that war to a victorious end. It has been contended that the calm which the President preserved in his two years of difficult negotiations with Germany, his efforts to secure peace, even "without victory," his admirable speeches, and his strong notes to the German Government served a purpose to prepare us for war and to reconcile us to it. Undoubtedly they did. What would have happened had we been less patient and long-suffering, had we supported our protests against German barbarism with a great preparation for military movement, is a matter on which opinions differ. War might have been avoided—that is a pure surmise. Had we intervened earlier the war would be over to-day—that is another pure surmise. We do know that when the war came to them the American people, unprepared though they were, accepted it with a surprising unanimity of purpose to carry it through.

We had been told that there lay a possibility of trouble among our millions of citizens of German birth and descent, and the aliens in our country. The great number of them have proved absolutely loyal. It is true that in some localities largely settled by these people there were made feeble attempts at protest and obstruction, but these were quickly conquered by the general outburst of patriotism. Those at heart disloyal were quick to realize their danger and to shape their conduct so as to keep themselves within the law. Against the really dangerous aliens and disloyal citizens the government was quick to act, and within twenty-four hours after war was declared thousands of

them were safe behind the bars. The prompt
and effective work of the Secret Service, supported by local police, prevented outbreaks of
any kind. The hopes and plans of Germany
for wide-spread disorders blocking our preparation for hostilities were blasted, and to-day it is
a common thing to see in German newspapers
bitter comment on what they deem the supine
attitude of the Germans in America—traitors
to the Fatherland. If there were dangerous
efforts at obstruction anywhere, they were in
Congress, made by a few short-sighted pacifists,
who could not see that America had to fight if
she was to keep her liberty, and by timid politicians who pandered to the pro-German senti-
ments of their constituents. Even these trimmed
their sails when they found how the wind blew.

The administration realized the danger, and
once the die was cast set itself with all vigor to
meet it. For the fight we had ready a navy in
weight of gun-power rated then third in the
world, and manned by a personnel than which
there is none better. But in a military force
with which to engage effectively in so great a
conflict we were woefully lacking. Our regular

army on April 1, 1917, consisted of 5,791 officers and 121,797 men; the National Guard available for federal service numbered 3,733 officers and 76,713 enlisted men, and there were in the army reserve approximately 4,000 enlisted men. This made a total armed force of approximately 212,000, a number utterly inadequate for the conflict ahead.

The problem faced by the country was a mighty one. Briefly stated, these were its main elements:

To strengthen our navy, that it could meet and whip unaided the navy of Germany.

To raise an army of at least 5,000,000 men, well trained and equipped.

To bridge the sea with ships that we might transport these men to the battle-front and maintain a steady flow of food and munitions for our own and our allies' use.

To stimulate the production of food and munitions, that we might fill the shortage in our allies' lands.

To raise by taxation and loans more money than had been spent by our government since the beginning of its history.

Time pressed. The collapse of all orderly government in Russia meant a threat of increased German armies on the western front. Our allies were calling to us for food, money, men, and munitions. Fortunately for us, their armies held the enemy rigidly, while we prepared to send them succor in an ever-increasing flow.

In a military way we had one great asset, our munition-factories. During the years of our neutrality, answering the demands of Great Britain, France, Russia, and Italy, private enterprise had developed on an enormous scale plants for the manufacture of guns of all sizes, shells, and high explosives—everything, in fact, needed for the equipment of an army. These were at our government's disposal, and those who manned them, from manager and engineer to the workmen at the lathe and forge, became a part of our great patriotic army of defense. Then, too, we had wisely, by government and private enterprise, laid the foundations of a great merchant marine.

Every element in the problem was vital to its solution—army, navy, food, transport, and finance—but when we found ourselves at war the most immediately pressing question was that of shipping. Manifestly it was impossible for us to conduct a war overseas if we did not have the vessels in which to transport the soldiers and, moreover, our allies were sorely beset by the ravages of the enemy submarines, and were in grave danger from lack of food, fuel, and metal. The Germans' unrestricted submarine warfare was working havoc with the world's merchant marine, and at the moment when America became a belligerent, German piracy was on the high wave of success. Ships were being sunk at the average rate of more than 600,000 gross tons a month. In the month of April, alone, 893,877 gross tons of the world's merchant fleet were sent to the bottom. There were but two ways to overcome this menace: to conquer the submarines and to build ships. The first warlike act of our government was to send our navy to help our allies combat the pirates of the underseas.

CHAPTER III

THE SHIPPING PROBLEM

IN discussions of the shipping problem much misunderstanding often results from a confusion of the terms of ship register. The ton-register of a ship, used by all maritime nations, is 100 cubic feet. The gross tonnage of a vessel is the sum in cubic feet of all its enclosed spaces divided by 100.

The net tonnage is the gross tonnage less certain deductions on account of crew quarters, engine-room, water-ballast, and other spaces not used for passengers and cargo.

The dead-weight tonnage, or carrying capacity, is the number of long tons (2,240 pounds) of cargo and bunker-coal that the vessel is capable of carrying when loaded to the load water-line.

Displacement tonnage is the number of tons of sea-water displaced by the vessel when charged to the load water-line.

The dead-weight tonnage of a vessel can be obtained by multiplying the gross tonnage by 1.6.

At the beginning of the war, in 1914, according to the best available figures, there were in the world 45,403,877 gross tons of steam-vessels and 3,685,675 net tons of sailing vessels. Figuring gross for steam and net for sail, this gave a total tonnage of 49,089,552. Of the steam-vessels, Great Britain and her allies owned 23,638,966 gross tons, and of the sailing, 1,131,-463 net tons, a total of 24,770,429. At the same date the United States had on the seas, the Great Lakes, and in the Philippines steamers of a gross tonnage of 4,330,078, and sailing ships of a net tonnage of 1,038,116, a total of 5,368,194. Of this American tonnage but a small part was fit for foreign trade.

It must be remembered, also, that of the world tonnage not a little part consisted of small vessels unfitted for overseas carrying, and in reckoning the vessels available for the merchant service after the outbreak of the war, the tonnage of Germany and her allies must be subtracted, for the greatest number of these vessels had found refuge in home and neutral harbors.

The British Isles in peace-times depend on

the world for more than one-half of their food, and this has to be carried to them by the seas. Great Britain is, in fact, dependent on her shipping for her life. When millions of her men had to be taken from her farms, her factories, and her mines to fight her battles, this condition was intensified. She had to import from every quarter of the world vast quantities of materials, both raw and manufactured, to be used in her defense against the Hun. Increasing the strain on her shipping, she had to transport large armies to the battle-fronts in France, in Mesopotamia, the Balkans, and South Africa. France was in like case. She was not as dependent as Great Britain on the outside world for food, but the greater part of her coal and iron deposits were lost to her in the first rush of the Germans, and these losses had to be replaced from overseas. Italy's entrance into the war in 1915, while it added valiant armies to the cause of the Allies, put another burden on the world's carriers, for Italy has within her borders practically none of the raw materials needed for the prosecution of so great a conflict. Germany was quick to see this weak spot in her enemies' armor. If she could drive theirs and neutral merchantmen from the seas, she would stop the flow of food and munitions into their countries, and quickly bring them to a disastrous peace. It was for this that she began her lawless submarine warfare, and risked the hostility of America. She underestimated the courage of America. She underestimated the power of America. Granted that America would fight, how was she to bridge those 3,000 miles of sea? So laughing at America's protests against her barbarity, Germany's submarines began the destruction not only of her enemy's shipping but of the shipping of the neutral world.

The damage done to the world's shipping from the beginning of the war to the end of 1917 is shown in the following table, issued by the British Government:

	BRITISH	FOREIGN	WORLD
Losses, in gross tons, through enemy action and marine risks.	7,097,492	4,730,080	11,827,572
Gains—new construction.......	3,031,555	3,574,720	6,606,275
Enemy tonnage captured.......	780,000	1,809,000	2,589,000
Total.....................	3,811,555	5,383,720	9,195,275
Net loss to the world...............................			2,632,297

The losses in the first quarter of 1918 were 1,123,310 tons. Did they continue at that rate the yearly loss would be more than 4,000,000 tons.

For the whole period the figures might not seem so startling, but the full menace is clearer when we find that more than one-half of the sinkings occurred in 1917, following Germany's announcement of unrestricted warfare. By quarters the losses in that year were: 1,619,373; 2,236,934; 1,494,473; 1,272,843. It is seen that the apex of destruction was reached about the time of America's entry into the war.

The danger was great. The continued loss of more than 5,000,000 tons yearly, if not offset, would soon separate us from our allies and leave them in dire distress. A chart issued by the British Government shows graphically how the danger has been met. The curve showing the world's loss of ships by months holds fairly steady until the third quarter of 1916, when it rises with startling abruptness, reaching its highest point in April, 1917, in which month 893,877 gross tons were destroyed; it falls away as abruptly to December, when 452,063 tons were lost. Struggling after it, but below it, is the curve showing the world's output of new vessels. At the close of the last year there was still a wide gap between them. But America's new shipyards were not then in full operation. They are to-day, and those lines will cross, to Germany's discomfort.

When we entered the war there were under the American flag hardly 2,000,000 gross tons of merchant shipping available for the heavy overseas work required. Nearly all of this was employed in the Great Lakes and coastwise trade. We had to send great armies to Europe. It is estimated that to move one soldier to France and to keep him supplied with food and equipment requires a carrying capacity of five dead-weight tons constantly on the sea, so that to transport an army of 1,000,000 men to the battle-ground and keep them there demanded a carrying capacity of 5,000,000 dead-weight tons. Little wonder that the Germans made light of America as a belligerent and predicted confidently that their submarines would be able to keep our armies at home.

When it became evident in the fall of 1916

that because of the demands and ravages of the war there was threatened a dangerous shortage of merchant vessels for even our ordinary peaceful commerce, our government acted to overcome the difficulty. On September 17 the Federal Shipping Act was passed, forming the United States Shipping Board, with two functions—the first, in time of peace to promote the development of our merchant marine; the second, in event of war, to meet the shipping problems that might arise. To carry out the second task, after we had entered the war the Emergency Fleet Corporation was organized for the purpose of constructing the needed vessels. To-day the Fleet Corporation is building the vessels and the Shipping Board is operating them.

The early history of the Shipping Board is not one of great accomplishment. Plans were made and foundations laid, but there was a great deal of delay in the pressing work caused by disagreements among the five members. Valuable time was wasted in controversies over designs for the ships, and the frequent changes in the personnel of the board by resignations

further impeded the work. Of the first board
the chairman, William Denman, a San Fran-
cisco lawyer, held on longest, until July, 1917.
He and General George W. Goethals, of Panama
Canal fame, then head of the Fleet Corporation,
became engaged in a controversy over the types
of ships to be built and methods, which bid fair
to delay dangerously the whole programme.
President Wilson settled the matter by securing
the resignations of both men. General Goethals
was subsequently placed at the head of the
quartermaster's department of the army. The
early experiences of the board made it plainly
evident that if its great work was to be carried
on successfully it must have at its head an able
business man and organizer. One of the cheering things about the conduct of the war has
been the promptness with which our leaders of
industry have answered the government's call
to service, abandoned all other pursuits that
the country might have the benefit of their experience. In this case the President sent for
Edward N. Hurley, of Illinois, a man accustomed to business operations on a large scale,
and from the moment he took charge new im-

petus was given to the work, and the record of
the board's accomplishment has become one of
the marvels of industry.

The early programme called for the construction of vessels of an aggregate of 13,000,000
dead-weight tons. This meant more than 1,850
passenger, cargo, refrigerator ships and tank-
ers of between five and twelve thousand tons.
As the war went on and the submarine continued its ravages, as our military plans were
enlarged and it was seen that we must put
immense armies in the field, our ship-building
plan had to be greatly increased and pushed
with a vigor well-nigh superhuman. To conduct this operation Charles M. Schwab, the
steel manufacturer, was called on, and under
his direction as head of the Fleet Corporation
great strides have been made in the construction work.

When in 1916 the Shipping Board began its
work, there were in the United States only 37
steel shipyards, with 162 ways, and these were
running at full capacity, 70 per cent of their
work being on naval vessels. We had 24 wooden
shipyards, with 73 ways, but these were almost

defunct. The number of men employed in these yards was 45,000, and in that year 600,000 dead-weight tons of ships were built. But it was estimated that now 6,000,000 tons a year was the minimum we must have. To secure them existing yards had to be enlarged, new yards built, expert ship architects and operating heads obtained. More difficult was the labor problem. Ship mechanics were scarce and wooden ship-building was almost a lost art. A great labor army had not only to be enlisted but trained. The carrying of material from the source to the water-front involved great traffic difficulties. But the work is being done. The United States has to-day the greatest ship-building machine in the world. In 1917 it produced 1,400,000 dead-weight tons of shipping. It is expected that in the current year nearly 5,000,000 tons will leave the ways. Between January 1 and August 24, 535 vessels, totalling 2,923,973 dead-weight tons, were launched.

By July, 1918, there were in operation 158 shipyards on the Atlantic and Pacific coasts and the Great Lakes. The ways numbered more than 750, of which 398 were for steel, 332 for wooden, and 10 for concrete and composite vessels. The men employed were over 300,000. Day after day the ships were slipping into the water. On the national holiday the world heard "the big splash," when nearly 100 steel and wooden vessels, adding a dead-weight tonnage of 474,464 to our merchant fleet, were launched with patriotic demonstrations. By this date we had increased our merchant marine to a carrying capacity of nearly 10,000,000 dead-weight tons. Of these 730,176 were obtained by the seizure of interned enemy ships. They had been damaged, but were quickly repaired and placed in service.

This is fine evidence of American ingenuity and energy. Such a record could only be accomplished by wise direction and the whole-hearted co-operation of every man engaged in the task. Hundreds of business men and engineers left their peace-time occupations to help the government in this vital work. Thousands of workmen gave up accustomed labor in familiar surroundings and travelled far to learn a new trade and do their bit in the war. Most of these men were unskilled and had to be trained. To train them it was necessary to have competent instructors, and these were lacking, so schools were established where skilled mechanics fitted others to go into the yards and teach ship-building. To secure whole-souled work a campaign of patriotic appeal has been carried on and every man engaged made to feel that his is a vital part in the cause of liberty.

The speed in construction that has been attained would not have been possible under the old methods. The government had to resort to the standardization of designs, and, as it is called, to fabrication. Under the old method nearly every part of the ship was made in the yard. The frames and plates were cut, bent, and fitted. Under the new system the parts of the ship may be made at a dozen widely separated places. They are of standard sizes and are shipped to the assembling-point, the yard, and are fitted together with great rapidity. A completed hull will be launched; it is hardly in the water before the cranes swing over the empty ways, and in fifteen minutes a new keel will be in place. Neither time nor motion are wasted in our shipyards. The steel collier *Tuckahoe*, of 5,550 dead-weight tons, was launched on the Delaware on May 4, twenty-seven days after her keel was laid, and ten days later she was ready for sea. This record was later broken.

This great programme of ship fabrication of necessity put a strain on the mills of the country. These mills were already overcrowded with war orders, and to meet the new demand were obliged to enlarge their production capacity. Coincident with the construction of the new yards arrangements had to be made to secure a greatly increased output of turbines and engines, and this meant the making of the special tools of all kinds required in the engine-shops. The work was done. There was an early shortage of engines, but now this has been overcome. The existing steel-mills could not supply the plates fast enough, and three new mills had to be built to make up the shortage. The programme for building each year 604 wooden ships of the Ferris type, of 3,500 tons dead-weight, was delayed four months by the difficulty of securing proper lumber. When the

board found it had to rake the country to get
the large timbers required, it stopped the building of additional wooden ways and contented
itself with a more modest programme.

A few years ago, before the exigencies of war
came upon us, the building of the Hog Island
assembling-yard would have been considered of
itself a big undertaking. On the swampy banks
of the Delaware, below Philadelphia, there was
built in less than a year a manufacturing city.
The major part of this work was done in the
hardest winter we have known in a long time,
when not only bitter weather but a railroad
blockade and a fuel famine were hampering industry. The land had to be drained, roads
built, ways, shops, and even homes constructed
for thousands of workmen. What was done
there has been duplicated in many other places,
and so great has been the success of the work
that in three of the new assembling-yards, those
at Hog Island, and Bristol on the Delaware,
and on Newark Bay, more vessels will leave the
ways in one year than all the English yards
have ever been able to build in the same time,
and hitherto England has been the greatest

ship-building country in the world. Mr. Hurley
estimates that between April 6, 1917, and
June 1, 1918, the Shipping Board had added to
the shipping under its control nearly 4,500,000
dead-weight tons. This was done by new
construction, by the seizure of enemy vessels,
by the requisitioning of 86 Dutch vessels, and
by the charter of 215 vessels from neutral countries. The quantity production of ships did
not begin until January of this year, and since
then the output has been increasing month by
month. He estimates, further, that in 1919,
with 751 ways in operation, averaging each three
vessels of 6,000 tons a year, we should turn
out in that year fully 13,500,000 tons. This
rate of construction would give us by the end
of 1920 the largest merchant marine in the
world. To man this great fleet the Shipping
Board has established schools for officers and
seamen. In this work of training it spends
monthly $250,000.

There is a race between the submarine and
the shipbuilder, but the figures show how the
latter is winning. In the first six months of
the present year 2,089,393 gross tons of Allied

and neutral shipping were sunk. In the same period America and Great Britain constructed ships of 2,133,591 gross tonnage. There was still a wide margin to overcome. But the American output of shipping in May was three times that of January, and was steadily increasing. By the middle of July vessels were being delivered to the Shipping Board at the rate of nearly four for each working-day, a daily output of 20,461 dead-weight tons, or 12,788 gross tons. Moreover, the increasing efficiency of the naval fight against the submarine was telling.

By the gallantry of our navy and the navies of our allies, and by the energies of the ship-builders of America and Great Britain has been overcome the lawless and murderous submarine campaign on which Germany staked her hopes of victory. To-day a steady line of vessels travels the sea lane, bearing our thousands of soldiers to the battle-front, and carrying succor to our hard-pressed allies.

CHAPTER IV

THE CANTONMENTS

THE second "contemptible little army" that Germany had to face was the American. The first was the British. England, not having heeded the warnings of Lord Roberts and other men of his vision, could throw into France hardly 150,000 men to meet the first onslaught of the Germans. Having shown like lack of vision, despite the pleas of men like Theodore Roosevelt and Leonard Wood, and in spite of the tragic events in Europe, it took us two years longer to see the German menace, and we were unprepared to meet it. So coincident with the vast work of bridging the sea, we had to find the men to send across, to train them into soldiers, and to make the arms with which they were to fight. On the declaration of war we had a regular army of some 127,000 men fit for the battle-front, and about 80,000 national guardsmen, patriotic men who had volunteered for service, but were only partly trained. The government had to act quickly and wisely. It did so. First, recruiting was stimulated by a patriotic campaign to bring the Regular Army and the National Guard up to the then authorized war strength of 287,000 and 450,000 respectively. But this did not give us the force needed. The selective-draft act was passed and enforced, the industry of the country was speeded up to make the arms and equipment. Within a year we had under arms 1,652,725 officers and men. Within seventeen months 1,500,000 of these were in France and hundreds of thousands of our soldiers were in the front line of battle, conducting themselves with a gallantry that stirred the heart of every American. By their bravery, their alertness, and resourcefulness they had won the unstinted commendation of the war-tried soldiers of France and Great Britain.

We have heard much of delays and mistakes in the conduct of the military administration. Undoubtedly they have occurred. It took time to get the right men in control of the machinery. The airplane programme broke down lamentably. The ordnance programme was unduly delayed. At one time, as a member of the administration said recently, our war machinery almost ceased to function. The mistakes were rectified, many new and able men were called in to aid in the war administration, and by the middle of this year the machinery was working with fair smoothness. Airplanes and guns were coming from the factories in quantities, and our armed men were going over seas in a steady flow.

Our Navy Department has done its work so smoothly since the war began that there has been a tendency to compare its operations with that of our Department of War. One is apt to forget the difference in the problems presented. The navy was a going concern. As our first line of defense it had always been a pet of Congress. When the conflict came its expansion was necessary, but in nothing like the degree that was required for our neglected army. The War Department was organized to care for about 250,000 men. Suddenly the work of handling at least fifteen times that number was thrown upon it. It is not to be wondered that we had hesitation and trying delays.

It was early seen that for the conflict an army of at least 3,000,000 men would be needed. It was seen, too, that the difficulties of raising such a number by volunteers would be great. We had the experience of our own Civil War and the more recent experience of England to study. England came to the draft late in this war. Our government wisely accepted that method at once. Some members of Congress did balk at the selective-service law, but they did not succeed in delaying its passage for any time. The American people, said the pacifists, would never accept the principle of compulsory service. Under pressure of the administration, however, the selective-service law was passed in a surprisingly short time, considering its drastic change in our historic policy, and on May 18 the President signed it. The American people accepted it willingly. They saw the injustice of allowing one fit man to stay at home in security while another volunteered to give his life in the country's cause.

Here we had the beginning of our great National Army, which within a year of its formation was conducting itself gallantly on the battle-fields of France.   Its success was due to the wise policy of the administration and to the energy of those officers of our Regular Army on whom fell the heavy task of organizing and training it.   Under the law all men in the country between the ages of twenty-one and thirty-one years had to register, that their fitness and liability for military service might be determined.   On June 5 nearly ten million were enrolled by the boards which had been organized all over the country to conduct the draft.   The efforts to obstruct the work were few and contemptible.   Of this great number of registrants the boards classified 2,428,447 in Class A, comprising those who could be placed in the military service with the least disturbance to the industrial, agricultural, and domestic interests of the nation.   Every man was numbered, and the order of his call to service settled by a lottery drawn in Washington.   Before December 15 there were in the army 897,061 of these selected men, including delinquents reported as deserters.

Class A received an increase on June 5, 1918, of about 400,000 men, who had come of age in the course of the year. By August 1, 1918, 1,347,512 of these men were in the National Army. General E. H. Crowder, the provost marshal-general, who had charge of the conduct of the draft, estimated that 875,000 more would be called to service before the end of the year, and that there were available in the first class for fighting material 877,359 registrants. This narrow margin of hardly more than 2,000 indicated the necessity of either increasing the draft age or of raking the other classes already registered for the men sure to be needed. Congress, therefore, in August amended the law so as to make all men from 18 to 45 years of age liable for military service.

When the National Army was first planned we had at hand not enough officers to train and command it. The problem of obtaining them was difficult. Quick steps had to be taken to have them ready by the time the men were assembled. Fortunately, there had been held in the two summers preceding the war, through the enterprise of General Wood and a group of army officers and private citizens, a small series of training-camps from which could be obtained the nucleus of the great corps of officers needed. Now sixteen of these camps were organized in different parts of the country, and a three months' course of intensive training given to volunteers. From them came nearly 50,000 young men who had qualified for commissions in the various arms of the service. Thus was the personnel of our new military force provided for.

Coincident with this great work there had to be accomplished one of the most difficult tasks that had ever fallen to the War Department. No places were ready where the new armies could be trained. We were embarked on an enterprise of unknown possibilities. Not a million but millions of soldiers might be needed, and this meant the organization of huge and permanent military schools. We had provided the method and the machinery for getting the men. Now we had to prepare the means of training them. The General Staff of the army had foreseen that such a contingency might arise, and had prepared before the war a general scheme to meet it. They had designed a standard cantonment capable of sheltering what was then an army division, 36,000 men. The plan was very simple. On it the buildings for the various units were stretched along in a straight line, regiment after regiment, with their barracks, officers' quarters, hospitals, and stables arranged on a single street, so designed that it could be cut and twisted to suit the conformation of any site. The War Department needed thirty-two of these cantonments, sixteen to house an increased National Guard, and sixteen for the coming National Army. Congress promptly appropriated the money asked, some $79,000,000, but when the work of letting the contracts began, it was found that so greatly had the price of labor and material increased since the plan was made, there were not sufficient funds. It was therefore decided to place the sixteen National Guard divisions under canvas in the South, and to construct the more permanent quarters for the National Army. To build sixteen cities, with every house provided with electric light, running water, and heat, in the three months allotted, was a task to strain any organization. In this case it fell to the construction branch of the quartermaster's department, consisting of a colonel, two captains, and a stenographer. That useful body, the Council of National Defense (of which I shall speak later), was turned to for aid. The council formed an emergency construction committee and sent a call for men skilled in town-planning, for engineers, for experts in water-supply and sewage-disposal, landscape-architects, and builders. The best in the country hurried to Washington and rendered patriotic service. Many of them served without pay. Others received commissions in the army. All worked, without ceasing, to have the cantonments ready by September 1, and with few exceptions they succeeded.

After the work was authorized the choosing of the sites took time. Consideration had to be given to many elements of the problem. The camps had to be located near large centres of population, with good railroad facilities at hand; the ground had to be capable of proper drainage, and a great water-supply available. In every case at least 2,000 acres of land were needed to give space for 1,400 buildings, manœuvring-grounds, and rifle-ranges. June had half passed before the last site had been settled on, and July was at hand when the last contract for construction was let. There was no time for the taking of competitive bids. The work had to be put in the hands of the great contracting firms who had the machinery to handle it, and they did it on a cost-plus-a-commission basis, with their profit being limited to $250,000. This method, while designed to save the government money, had in reality quite the opposite effect, for the contractors, being limited in their profit and being called on for the highest possible speed in construction, had little reason for economy in labor or material. But however high the cost, the work was done, and on September 5 the first increments of the new army were moving into the soldier towns.

The first call for service in the National Army brought 687,000 men to the colors. Beginning in September, they were sent to the cantonments in successive increments. They found waiting there officers to train them, and for many a life of more comfort, health, and interest than they had ever known. Then began the work of our greatest schools of Americanism and democracy. Rich man and poor man, business man, laborer, farmer, and mechanic bunked side by side, ate the same food, wore the same uniform, and performed the same duties. In six months they were welded into a patriotic and efficient army. No praise is too high for the officers who led in this great task or for the men who seconded them by their readiness to learn and to serve. Most of these men had known nothing of military life; thousands of them nothing of the healthy life of out-of-doors; there were among them men who were discontented with the fate that had fallen to them, but even of these the greater part soon found contentment in the new environment; before the winter of training was over the shirkers were few in number.

We in New York saw the procession of our selective-draft men march up Fifth Avenue on the eve of their departure for Camp Upton. Men from the banks and offices, men from the stores and shops, moved along in straggling lines, and out of step, cheerful and cheering, and yet a motley body. Of many of them pale faces, stooping shoulders, and shuffling gait

Marching out to dine after short period of training at one of the National Army cantonments.

told the story of sedentary living.   They looked as though but little hardship would break them. They did not seem the stuff of which soldiers could be made.   Six months later we saw them march again on Fifth Avenue on a bitter day. A miracle seemed to have been worked.   Brown and hard, clean-limbed, they swung along, bodies erect, heads up, in perfect step and alignment.   You were conscious of their pride in their uniform, in the task they had accomplished, and of their part in the greater task that lay ahead of them.   To-day they are overseas and many of them have paid the great price that must be paid if men are to be free.

The material with which the War Department had to work in forming the first divisions of the National Army was very raw, and it came not in driblets through recruiting-stations, so that it could be readily absorbed in trained units, but it came in mass.   Besides, there was the widest possible divergence in the character of the men.   Every nationality was represented, even to Turks and Chinese.   Of the whole fully 10 per cent could not speak English, and

in every cantonment there were at least a thousand who could not read or write. The cantonment became not only a camp but a school.
For the foreign-born, classes in English were
formed, and for the illiterate, classes in elemen-
tary studies. Schools, too, were established to
fit the more intelligent for different services in
which they were needed. There are a great
number of these services. The commander of
one of the camps had a list of nearly one thousand occupations for which specialists were
wanted for the army. It included dog-trainers.

Our National Army has been a success because neither energy nor money has been spared
in the care for the men in their early service.
The quarters are comfortable, electric-lighted,
and screened in summer, and in winter well
heated. Every man has his own cot, and is
amply provided with blankets and clothing.
The food is wholesome and plentiful, and the
active life in the open air gives a zest to the
appetite. The health and morals of the men
have been safeguarded in a degree never before
known in our military history. Liquor is taboo.
When you watch a company of these soldiers in

the crisp air of the early morning, swinging in rhythmic unison through the physical drills, you do not wonder at the erect and sturdy figures in khaki to be seen by the hundreds in our streets in these war-times.

The life of the soldier is not all work. From reveille to retreat there is a pretty steady round of drill and police duty, but let there be but a few minutes to spare and the grounds are alive with athletic games. At times you might think a cantonment just a great school for baseball, football, or basket-ball. In the evening, for relaxation, there are the theatre, the moving-picture show, the library, and the huts of the Y. M. C. A. and Knights of Columbus, with their variety of entertainment.

One afternoon last spring I watched a party of some two thousand recruits arrive at Camp Upton. When the long train had stopped they assembled quickly on the platform of the station, the men from each local board under the charge of an officer. They were from the factory towns and farms of New England and by their appearance represented varying degrees of worldly prosperity. There were bent little fel-

lows who had just come from the looms of Fall
River, and tall, raw-boned youths who had left
their ploughs and hoes among the stony hills.
Most of them were cheery, facing the new ad-
venture with good-will, and they started toward
the camp in a ragged formation, with much
shouting and waving of flags. A few of the
faces were gloomy, filled with apprehension of
the days ahead. One could not wonder, for it
is no light thing to leave your home and occu-
pation for the hardships of the camp and the
danger of the field. But a company of fresh-
men just arriving at college would have shown
a like proportion of set and solemn faces. Some
of the men had little bags containing precious
possessions, which they hoped Uncle Sam would
allow them to take to France; others portman-
teaus with which they could have travelled
around the world; others had nothing in their
hands and wore neither hats nor coats; they
were stripped for action and trusted the government to give them all they needed. The
procession straggled across the plain and down
one of the long cantonment streets. From every
barrack-window came a volley of good-natured

gibes: "Hey, Sam, you won't look so chipper when you get the needle!" "Say, Alonzo, why don't you call your vally to carry your kit?" "Oh, nurse, nurse, come quick; there's Jimmy running away to war with ma's knitting-bag." The men in khaki had forgotten that not so long since they had shuffled down this same street in this same way.

The motley procession crossed a parade-ground and there divided, the improvised companies being led off to their quarters. It was the time for retreat, and as the rookies squatted on the ground before their barracks, resting tired limbs, the band on the parade-ground sounded the first notes of "The Star-Spangled Banner." Instantly the life of the camp stopped. Every moving figure in khaki halted and stood at attention, facing the headquarters on the hilltop a mile away, where the flag flew from its tall mast.

From every side came shouts: "Stand up, you men, face toward the flag—hats off!"

They got to their feet with expressions of wonderment on their faces and stood bare-headed until the last notes of the national an-

them died away and the flag fluttered down.
It was their first lesson in army life.

A few days later I saw these same men.
They were in uniform and every man of them
was shaved and scrubbed. Under the orders of
a martinet of a "non-com" they were keeping
good step and executing squads right and
squads left with fair precision.

Great melting-pots—so our cantonments have
been justly called. In them thousands of our
foreign-born have become true Americans.
They have learned the language of America
and the ideals of America and have turned willing soldiers in her cause. That this is true is
shown by the great number of foreign-born men
who were called to the army under the selective-
service law, and have since become naturalized
as citizens. By act of Congress this process
was rightly made easy for them. In one afternoon at Camp Upton I saw 300 men forswear
old-time allegiances and become citizens of the
United States. Among them were men of every
nationality. There were Russians and Poles,
Danes and Swedes, citizens of the British Empire and the French Republic. Among them

there were a score of Germans and Austro-Hungarians. Again, in our cantonments class feeling has been swept aside, for the selective-service law showed no favoritism. Its provisions called to service rich and poor alike, and so they have come to understand one another better. The only class distinction known in the new army comes through intelligence and merit. The men called as privates have their opportunity to win commissions. Training-schools have been established for them and many have proved themselves worthy to wear the officers' insignia.

These cantonments have given their lesson not only to those who have served in them but to the whole country. The bugaboo of militarism has been laid low. We are not willing to accept the German brand of militarism that makes for conquest and Kultur. But a militarism that strengthens the country's manhood and trains and fits it to defend its homes and fight for justice has proved its worth. Every community over the land has seen its young men called to service by the law. Many of them answered with reluctance and with rebel-

lion in their hearts. The same communities have
seen those men months later, upstanding in
their uniforms, improved in physical and mental vigor and imbued with a new sense of patriotism and desire for service. They have seen
what our kind of militarism has done for our
men. America has been caught once unprepared to fight. She will not be so again. One
feels confident that when peace comes there will
be a wide-spread demand that the work of our
cantonments be continued and that we do not
abandon these great schools for the discipline
and improvement of our manhood.

Only by a visit to one of the cantonments
can a conception be had of the magnitude of
the work which the government has done and
is doing. They are all cut to the same pattern,
generally being laid out in a great U. An example of the best of them is Camp Dix at
Wrightstown, New Jersey. Going by train
through a quiet farming country, you pass into
a deep railroad cut, and when you emerge from
it you have suddenly before your eyes a great,
busy city. You enter it by a wide, clean road.

At one hand you see the great "hostess house," managed by patriotic women for the entertainment of the soldiers' visitors. Beyond that, stretching for a long mile on either hand, are the barracks of the men, set in broad, open spaces. The striking note is the absolute cleanliness—not a scrap of paper, not a bit of rubbish to be seen anywhere. The traffic on the road is heavy. There is a constant movement of wagons and motors, but it is carefully regulated by the military police at the crossings. From headquarters hill, in the camp's centre, you see the whole place under your eyes, a great U of buildings, two miles in depth, enclosing the broad drill-grounds. There is life everywhere. The drill-grounds are alive with men. Here a company working at the manual of arms; here one swinging through the physical drill; here an awkward squad, not yet in uniform, learning the rudiments of marching.

The routine of the enlistment is rather complicated. First we go to the big hall where the recruits are received on their arrival. Here the records of the local draft boards are checked up and the men accounted for. Then they have

their physical examination. A small percentage
are rejected as unfit. A large percentage are
found to have remediable defects, and provision
is made for their treatment. Fully 2 per cent,
we were told, have the unpleasant but much-
needed experience of being fumigated, and all
have a good bath. Thence the recruit goes
to the personnel-office, where hundreds of soldier-
clerks are at work at long desks. The journey
from end to end takes a half-hour. Multiple records are made out for the War Department,
the camp-office, and the company commander.
These records give a condensed history of the
recruit, show his marks of identification and
his qualifications for special duties. When they
have been completed, he makes his allotments
of pay and files his application for government
insurance. He leaves the building a member
of the army and gets his uniform.

While we were watching this process, scores of
men moving from clerk to clerk down the long
line, our guide, an upstanding young soldier,
informed the captain in charge that one recruit
that day had refused to sign any papers. To
our inquiry as to what would be done in such a

case the soldier said: "He'll go to the guard-house. One of the officers will give him a pleasant talking to, reason with him, and the chances are he will come around to-morrow—most of them do. And when they do they get to like the life—it's a fine life."

CHAPTER V

MILITARY PREPARATION

LONG before the first increments of our National Army were called to the colors, our soldiers were pouring into France. Within three weeks after we declared war, missions from France and England, headed by General Joffre and Mr. Balfour, were in our country. The first thing they asked for was men, if only a division, to strengthen the morale of the Allied armies by the visible evidence that armed America was coming to their aid. This request was promptly granted, and on June 26 a division of our Regular Army landed in France. We had available for active service when war came only our Regular Army of 127,588 officers and men. In physique and morale, there was no finer body in the world, but their number was inadequate to make an impression on the battle-front. Under the national-defense act the government had power to call into service the National Guards of the various States, numbering then about 80,000 officers and men. The personnel of these troops was fine, all the men being volunteers, but they were neither hardened nor well trained. A part of them had seen service in the previous year on the Mexican border, but the work for which they were now needed was of a different character. By recruiting, the Regular Army was increased in a year to 513,840 officers and men, and to-day exceeds that number. The recruiting for the federalized National Guard was not so successful. Thousands who would otherwise have volunteered were deterred by the operation of the selective-service law. Some of the units could not be filled by volunteers and had to be brought to war strength by the breaking up of other organizations. A number of the Guard regiments received large increments from the National Army camps. But we find at the end of the first year of war the strength of the National Guard was 448,476 officers and men. Besides these troops and the National Army there was in the federal service a reserve corps of 96,210 officers and 77,360 men.

America could not choose the battle-ground

against Germany. The battle-front was in France and it was imperative that our armies get to it with all possible speed and in the greatest possible numbers. There were three elements in the problem which had to be nicely balanced. The programme of man-power had to be carried on without upsetting the munition programme. Both of these programmes had to be adjusted to that of tonnage. We have seen how the men were gathered. The Regular Army was started overseas with great promptness. General Pershing, who was to command abroad, arrived in Paris with his staff on June 13. Following the first contingent of troops, there was a steady movement of soldiers overseas. A division of the National Guard and a division of marines went early, with regiments of engineers, railroad men, and foresters. On these last fell the work of preparing the port of debarkation for the thousands who were to follow, and of building lines of communication to the training-camps inland and to the front. All the fighting units, even those of the Regular Army, have had to be schooled in the modern methods of warfare, and at least four months' training behind the lines are required before the troops can be sent into action. It was October 10, 187 days after war was declared, before our men were on the firing-line.

Meantime the work at home was pushed with vigor, but it was hampered by our lack of mobilization-camps. For nearly five months the whole National Guard could not be called into service because there were no training-camps ready for them. The idea of constructing for them cantonments like those of the National Army had been abandoned early, and in September they were mobilized under canvas in sixteen camps in the South. Here they worked hard through the winter in preparation for the contest ahead, and before the spring had come they were most of them in France. Following them promptly went the first divisions of the National Army, and by July 4 Secretary Baker was able to announce that we had more than 1,200,000 soldiers on or near the battle-front. By late July our men were in action in larger numbers than ever before in our history, and we were hearing daily of their deeds of gallantry.

This great movement of troops over the submarine-infested Atlantic is of the highest credit to the War Department and to the navy that guarded it so effectively. Considering the numbers involved the loss of life was remarkably small. But one loaded transport, the *Tuscania*, was lost during the year, and several hundred men went down with her. The movement was made possible by the co-operation of our allies, Great Britain and France, who turned over to us many of their vessels for the carrying of the men.

While the man-power programme has worked with admirable smoothness, the same cannot be said of the munition programme in the early part of the war. There were delays which were the subject of much criticism in Congress and elsewhere. A lack of co-ordination and too much experimentation were the cause. Then, too, in the early part of the war the right men were not in the right place. A marked improvement came when the government called to its service able business men like Edward R. Stettinius and John D. Ryan. The first was made an assistant secretary of war in charge of munitions, and the last was given the direction of aircraft production. Had they been in these places of responsibility earlier we should not have seen nearly a year go by before machine-guns and aircraft were coming from the factories in quantities.

When you have a mad dog in your yard you do not go out to find an improved rifle with which to shoot it. You use the one you have. When the war came we were lacking in guns of all kinds, from the light machine to the nine-inch heavy. We had at our disposal the Lewis machine-gun, an American invention, and other types which were being used with success on European battle-fields. Moreover, our factories had been making them for our allies in large quantities, and were prepared to make prompt deliveries. The Ordnance Department wanted something better, but instead of paralleling a programme of manufacture in large quantities of the other types with a programme of experimentation, it spent months in experimentation alone. The Browning guns, a splendid weapon, were the result. It was a year before they were being delivered in large numbers, and in the meantime we had to depend largely on our allies to equip our troops in France with such ordnance. The same process was followed in regard to the heavier guns. According to the evidence before the Senate Military Affairs Committee, efforts to improve details of the gun-carriages used by France, England, and Italy caused such a delay that the output of pieces of field-artillery this year will be very small, and we have been compelled to rely largely on the factories of our allies. It is true that they have been able to help us in this way because we have sent them large quantities of raw material and thousands of mechanics to work it into shape.

Once the machinery of the Ordnance Department did get in motion it worked with increasing momentum. We find that by May, 1918, the production of the modified Enfield rifle for the army had been speeded up to 45,000 a week. By the middle of August more than 100,-000 machine-guns of various types had been made, of which 19,100 were light Brownings and 11,200 of the heavy types. An ultimate yearly production was promised of 15,000 field-pieces of calibers ranging from 3½ to 9 inches.

Making cartridge-shells at the Bethlehem Steel Works.

"To a peace-time task of operating eleven government arsenals . . . the Ordnance Department added the supervision of several thousand factories engaged in the production of munitions of all kinds."

In criticism of the delays incurred in the Ordnance Department consideration must be given
to the size and complexity of the task which
confronted it.   When war was declared it had a
commissioned personnel of ninety-seven officers,
and was operating with a yearly expenditure of
about $14,000,000. The war programme re-
quired the expansion of its personnel to more
than 5,000 officers, and in the first year it
directed the expenditure of more than $4,500,-
000,000. To a peace-time task of operating
eleven government arsenals it had added the
supervision of several thousand factories engaged in the production of munitions of all
kinds. It had to develop industries hitherto
unknown in the country, such as that for reducing nitrate from the air.   For the manufacture
of gun-carriages on a large scale it had to create
organizations and build great shops. It constructed and is operating two large plants for
the making of high explosives, each of which
cost $45,000,000. Under its charge came the
development of new weapons of warfare of all
kinds and their production. The Browning gun
alone was a fine achievement. The heavy type

in a government test fired 20,000 shots in 48 minutes and 16 seconds, without malfunction.

The task this department has had to face has been one of the heaviest of the war. The number of items it has had to secure and supply to the troops will number at least 100,000, and they range from the firing-pin of a rifle to a sixteen-inch gun or a motor-truck. Fortunately it was able to draw into its personnel the best minds of industrial America. It has made mistakes. There have been trying delays at times, caused by hesitation and lack of initiative, but it can be said that by the end of the first year of war its direction and its methods had greatly improved, and that it was functioning smoothly.

The other great supply department of the army, the quartermaster's, has had a problem nearly as great, though not so intricate. Its work at the outbreak of the war had to be done quickly, as its first large task was to supply camps for the gathering armies. The department was at first handicapped by lack of money, since, because of obstructive tactics by the opponents of war, the Congress which adjourned on March 4 had failed to pass the army appropriation bill.

Red tape was cut; extraordinary care was taken in expenditures; money was borrowed from the appropriation for national defense; the Federal Reserve Board financed the contractors. The work was pushed rapidly, but it was not until June 15 that the new Congress made the needed appropriation. The making of the camps and cantonments has been described. But the department had to repeat these feats abroad, building in France great training and rest camps, and supplying buildings for the storage of vast quantities of war material.

To the subsistence division has fallen the feeding of the army, and its operations have been on a huge scale, and its purchases in a year run into hundreds of millions of pounds of staple foods of all kinds, and hundreds of millions of cans of vegetables and fruit. In the operations of the equipment division we notice purchases of such items as 75,000,000 yards of olive-drab cloth, 50,000,000 pairs of heavy stockings, 11,000,000 pairs of field-shoes, and 14,000,000 pairs of woollen breeches. The remount division, which has charge of the purchase, mobilization, and shipment of animals, spent nearly

$45,000,000 in one year. Great remount stations had to be established at all the camps, where the horses and mules could be assembled and put in condition before they were shipped to the war zone. It is estimated that in the army's operations one animal is needed for every five men. The mortality among these animals is very heavy, and constant replacement is required. With every 1,000,000 men we send abroad, at least 200,000 horses must go.

An idea of the multitude of smaller but none the less essential matters which require the War Department's attention can be had from an incident which occurred in Washington last winter. It was during the fuel famine, and the department appealed to the fuel administration for coal for a large candy-manufacturing company. Candy hardly seemed essential then. But inquiry developed the fact that this company was furnishing the government with cocoanut-shells in great quantities, and from them was obtained the fibre used in the respirators of gas-masks. Then there arose trouble in getting castor-oil. It is used as a lubricant in airplane motors, and the supply is limited. The government prepared to meet its needs by planting thousands of acres of land with castor-beans.

This vast work of equipping our army for war could not have been carried on with the success it has had it not been for the Advisory Commission of the Council of National Defense and its many subsidiary committees. These committees were composed of men representing every branch of our industry, and co-operated with the various military bureaus. Their function was at first purely advisory. But when any special article was called for they knew where it could be obtained or made in the least possible time. Mistakes were made. There were delays, as in the aircraft and gun production. In the rush of work sometimes important items seem almost to have been forgotten. For example, there was the problem of gas warfare. Our gas defensive was early provided for; not so the gas offensive. It was late in the spring of 1918 before we were ready to supply our armies abroad with gas-shells in the great quantities needed. It is no secret that the gas they are now using is the most effective known. Such defects in our war preparations seem to have been due to a lack of co-ordination. The country was stirred in the fall of 1917 when Senator Chamberlain of Oregon, in a public speech, charged the War Department with procrastination, and declared that it was not functioning properly. In Congress charges were made that our war programme had broken down. Whether or not they were fully justified is not the main issue now. Certain it is that their effect was salutary. The work was speeded up. Shifts were made among the bureau heads. New men were called in to supervise certain operations. More power was given to committees whose functions had hitherto been advisory. By the passage of the Overman bill by Congress in May of this year more power was given to the President as directing chief of all our war activities. Under its provisions he can make whatever administrative changes he wishes without hindrance from Congress. Under it the President has been able to secure the needed co-ordination in the gigantic task which the country has had to face. There is no divided opinion as to the necessity of accomplishing that task. The men of both the great political parties have heartily supported every move that promised victory, and the men of every industry have bent their energies to that end.

CHAPTER VI

THE MASTERY OF THE AIR

THE two most effective weapons used in the World War have been the machine-gun and the airplane. Both are American inventions. Yet when we declared war on Germany even the little army we had was insufficiently supplied with machine-guns, and possessed not a single fighting-plane. In April, 1917, the army air service consisted of 65 officers and 1,120 men. It had 300 second-rate planes and three small flying-fields.

It is a fact not generally known that even the Zeppelin had its forerunner in America, and that in the early nineties Congress appropriated $100,000 for the construction of a lighter-than-air machine. Its designer was a Doctor de Boussuet, a Frenchman, who planned a rigid balloon made of very thin steel plates, supported inside by light steel tubing. He was to obtain buoyancy by exhausting the air from the cylinder, and to propel it by the simple gas-engine of that day. All his figures as to strength and power were approved by naval engineers. It was designed to carry mail, but it was never built, because a disagreement arose between the government and its inventor as to his reward, should it prove a success. I can remember the doctor in his house in Brooklyn in 1896, sitting surrounded by a confusion of detail drawings, bewailing the stupidity of a government which was so parsimonious as to block his experiment, because of a matter of a few thousand dollars.

At that time Samuel P. Langley was experimenting in heavier-than-air machines. He was working on the correct principle of aeronautics —simply put, the faster you skate over thin ice the less is the likelihood of breaking through. He lacked satisfactory means of propulsion, yet in 1896 a model of his, driven by steam, did fly, and demonstrated the possibility of airplane navigation. In 1903 a model driven by a gas-engine made a prolonged flight, and he constructed the first man-carrying airplane. This he never succeeded in launching. Death ended his experiments. In 1914 Glenn Curtiss made a successful flight in that machine.

In the fall of 1907 Wilbur and Orville Wright came from Dayton, Ohio, to New York, seeking capital. They asserted that they had solved the flying riddle, but their claims were listened to somewhat sceptically in the quarters where they were heard. It was not until the next year when they went to France, and made extensive flights at low altitudes around French race-tracks, that the full measure of their success was realized by the world. In the summer of 1910 a little flying-school was established at Mineola, Long Island, on what is now the site of two great army fields, and it was a favorite afternoon diversion of Long Islanders to go there and watch a half-dozen aviators soaring around, hardly higher than the housetops. In the four years before the beginning of the Euro-pean War the development of aviation in this country was very slow. Such machines as we had were to be seen generally at county fairs, and what attention was paid to the aviation problem was by private individuals. Even up to the time of our entrance into the war the only indication that we had any air section in our army at all came from occasional reports of fatal accidents. Meantime abroad the science of airplane building and flying advanced with startling rapidity. The exigencies of war were the cause. From the primitive reconnoissance plane, the combatants went quickly to heavy-armed observation-planes, fitted with wireless and photographic apparatus, to very fast, high-flying, fighting-machines, and to large machines capable of carrying tons of bombs to spread devastation behind the battle-lines and in the cities. Systems of aerial acrobatics and combat were developed to a degree hitherto undreamed of. In none of these developments in military aeronautics did we follow. In all the years previous to April 6, 1917, we had spent just $1,500,000 in this branch of army service. We, in whose country the first plane had flown, had to sit humbly at the feet of our allies and learn. One trouble has been that our humility was not great enough.

It was believed that the armies that held the mastery of the air would win. Blind the Germans! It would be easier and quicker to send overseas an overwhelming air force than an overwhelming army. Though we had few aviators and no fighting-planes, we had thousands of young men ready and willing to train for flying, and great industrial plants to produce the machines rapidly. Then we had money. Congress quickly appropriated $640,000,000 to be available for the first year, and we began to work on our ambitious programme. This sum was later increased to over a billion dollars. The programme was not too ambitious. It was admirable. The disappointment came from our being made too sanguine of its first part being accomplished in a year. The American public and our allies were led to expect too much. There was too much talking. Who was responsible for this inflation of our expectations is a mooted question. The official Bureau of Public Information in its early career certainly had a way of issuing bombastic statements.

Within a year we were to have thousands of fighting-planes on the western front. How was this to be accomplished? The work was put in charge of a special board of the Signal Corps of the army working in conjunction with the newly formed Aircraft Production Committee of the Council of National Defense. This com-

mittee was made up of a number of men conspicuous as successful in the manufacture of
automobiles. There were fine engineers in both
of these bodies, but no experts in practical aeronautics.

Now consider their task. According to the
programme, to blind the German armies we
were to send to the western front as fast as possible at least 20,000 airplanes and aviators. It
was desired and expected that a large part of
these would be in service in the campaigns of
1918. The call for young men to train for aviation was sent out promptly, and they volunteered by thousands. As fast as they could be
cared for they were accepted for service. At
the time of our entry into the war we had in
the country but a small number of aircraft inventors and experts, and some dozen factories
which were making airplanes, or airplane parts
and accessories. Now aircraft companies began
to spring up like mushrooms and to prepare for
the work ahead. The main elements in the
problem faced were to secure quickly large
numbers of engines, material for the wings,
linen, cotton, wood, and navigating instru-

ments. The construction of engines and planes had to be carried on simultaneously. Our allies promptly placed at our disposal all their best models of engines and planes, and it might have seemed a wise thing to begin at once copying these and producing them as fast as possible. But it was believed that with our methods of manufacturing it would not be possible to produce such planes in the great numbers needed. It is a fact that we did not then have in the country enough expert mechanics to build in quantities engines as they are built abroad, that is by the most careful hand labor. Our mechanical labor has always been done largely by machinery. By a standardization of design and the use of machinery it would be possible to make engines in large numbers. So this method was adopted. We might have followed the two courses, copying the foreign engines with as much speed as possible, and at the same time experimenting with and perfecting our own. We did not, and time was lost.

In June the country was electrified by the announcement given out by the War Department, through the Bureau of Public Information, that American mechanical genius had invented an airplane engine which was superior to all others, and was, moreover, capable of being manufactured in great numbers by machine processes. Twenty-two thousand were promised within a year. We can smile now at that bombastic announcement. We recall the story which we were told of two engineers locking themselves in a few rooms in a Washington hotel and completing in three weeks designs for a motor which equalled, if not surpassed, in quality the best results of years of experiment and practice abroad. The inference was that our engineers went into those rooms with nothing in their heads but ideas, and emerged with working plans. As a matter of fact, as we know now, the engineers of a well-known automobile company, foreseeing our entry into the war, had been working for two years on the construction of an efficient airplane motor. Several models had been made and tested successfully on a block. The last, equipped with an air-propeller, had driven a truck about the streets of Detroit and had given proof of great power. It was on this design, which was offered to the govern-

ment, that the engineers worked, and they made
on it a number of changes and improvements
in their three weeks' conference. On July 3
the manufacturers were able to ship to Washington the first of the new engines, and it was
named the Liberty motor. To-day Liberty
motors are being built in large numbers, but
before they attained their present efficiency in
certain kinds of airplane work, months had to
be spent in experiment, and these months were
of vital importance in the war. The first motor
in block tests proved itself very powerful.
Weighing but little over 800 pounds, it developed 400 horse-power, giving it a weight of approximately two pounds per horse-power. In
practice on an airplane trouble developed. In
the design of airplane motors consideration has
to be given to the fact that they work in high
airs and changing temperatures, and their cool-
ing systems have to be so devised that they
function smoothly in changing altitudes. The
first Liberty motors did not do this, and changes
had to be made in the radiation system. Defects developed, also, in the lubrication, and
certain parts were found to be not sufficiently

strong.   The improvements added to the weight.
On September 12 Secretary Baker made a public announcement of the success of the final
tests and assured the country that a large number of motors would be ready for service in "a
comparatively short time."   The comparatively
short time proved to be nearly a year.

Contracts for the manufacture of the motors
were let to five large companies.   That there
should be no profiteering, these contracts provided that the manufacturers should receive a
profit of 12½ per cent on an estimated cost of
$5,000 per engine.   If the actual cost exceeded
$5,000 the manufacturer was to be reimbursed
for the outlay but would receive a reduced profit
or none at all; if the cost was less than $5,000
he was to receive a bonus of 25 cents on every
dollar saved.   While the percentage of profit
might seem large, it must be remembered that
the manufacturers had to provide special plants
and equipment in order to fill the orders.   Such
contracts would give assurance of profiteering
only by the most devious methods.   Certain of
the needed parts the manufacturers could not
make, and to obtain them they had to place

orders with numerous other plants. To equip
all these plants with the necessary machinery
took time, and once the quantity production
programme was started, more time was lost by
the constant changes in design ordered by the
Signal Corps. These changes were continued up
to April, and it was not until that month that
the production of motors had reached any
numbers. By June 1, instead of nearly the
20,000 promised, there had been delivered about
1,500. In that month, however, the factories
got into their stride, and week by week the output increased, so that by August the engines
were being delivered at a rate of nearly 1,000 a
week.

The delay in the aircraft programme was
known in Washington in the fall of 1917, and
this delay was due not only to the motor problem but to the plane construction. Apparently
little effective work was done to speed up. It
was not until the following April that the American public became aware of the trouble, and
explanations were demanded. Congress took
up the matter. It wanted to know why, when
it had provided for an expenditure of many

millions in one year so few machines had been produced, and we had sent no battle-planes abroad. It came out that of this money only $270,000,000 had actually been paid out, a large part of it for flying-fields, and that the rest was represented in contracts let and uncompleted. The men mainly responsible for the carrying out of the programme were called and questioned. Without doubt they were men of the highest patriotism and had acted with the best intentions, but it was felt in some quarters that serious mistakes had been made. Considerable acrimony developed. The President acted. He had hardly signed the Overman bill, on May 20, when he used its powers by ordering a sweeping reorganization. The production of aircraft was placed in the control of John D. Ryan, who had wide powers given him. The old Aircraft Production Board was continued in an advisory capacity. The control of aircraft operation was taken from the Signal Corps and placed with the newly organized Department of Military Aeronautics, which now has charge of all aerial work, of observation balloons and photography, as well as of the fighting-planes.

The original scheme for our airplane motor was an excellent one could it have been carried out in all its parts. It contemplated a standardized engine which could be produced in quantity and fitted to almost any kind of plane. The value of such a standardized engine at the battle-front is manifest. All the parts would be interchangeable and kept at hand, so that repairs could be quickly made. But experience has proved that the Liberty motor works well only in the heavier types of planes, such as those used in bombing and observation. It is very powerful for its weight, but its weight is too great for small fast-flying scout planes. A large number of these had been ordered, but it was found that the Liberty engine was too heavy and powerful for them. So for this special work we had to turn at a late date to types of motors originally offered to us by France, England, and Italy. Our air programme had to be materially altered. Our main task became to supply a great number of machines of the heavy type, for bombing, observation, and photography for our own use and the use of our allies. To our friends abroad we had to trust largely for equipment in the little single-seater fighters.

Even had the production of Liberty motors been accomplished on schedule time, it is doubtful that we should have had ready the planes on which to mount more than a small number. Without the planes the engines were useless. In the excitement tending the development of the motor other essential features of the programme were delayed. Millions of square yards of especially prepared cloths and millions of feet of carefully treated timber had to be secured for the construction of the wings. As every airplane carries some seven delicate instruments needed in its operation, the simultaneous production of thousands of these was a necessity. It was late in the summer of 1917 before these vital needs had been provided for.

The wood used in the construction of airplane wings has to be light, hard, straight-grained, and free from defects. Spruce has proved the best for the purpose, and of this wood our largest supply comes from the Northwest. Before we entered the war the Allied governments were buying spruce there in large quantities, but the added needs of our own war programme required that the government take over these outstanding contracts, assume control of the timber production, and supply the demands of all. At first the work of getting out the lumber was carried on in rather slipshod fashion. There were labor troubles during the summer and a subtle propaganda of disloyalty developed among the workers, hampering the operations. It was seen that it was necessary that the government not only supervise the spruce output, but that it operate the industry. In September the spruce production division of the army was formed and placed in charge of an officer, with headquarters at Vancouver. He organized a corps of officers, engineers, foresters, lumber-jacks, and mill-hands, numbering nearly 12,000 men. To counteract the insidious agitation of the I. W. W. an appeal to the patriotism of the workers was made. The Loyal Legion of Loggers and Lumbermen was formed in the forests and thousands of men enrolled in local chapters all over the lumber district. Labor disputes were satisfactorily settled, and disloyalty so stamped out that it ceased to be a menace. When the division was formed the forests and mills were putting out only 2,000,000 feet of lumber monthly, and 10,000,000 monthly were urgently needed. New methods had to be inaugurated; new roads had to be laid to reach distant stands of trees, and railroads constructed to get out the timber; new saw-mills had to be built and kilns provided for the drying of the spruce pieces. The task was difficult, but it was carried on with success. The production increased steadily month by month and the time spent in moving it across the continent to the factories was greatly reduced. By the summer of 1918 spruce in ample quantities was being obtained for our airplanes.

To provide the men to drive and care for these projected planes the War Department acted with promptness and energy. Great flying-fields were established all over the country and barracks and hangars were constructed in quick time. Within one year our air service was expanded until a personnel of some 1,100 officers and men became over 100,000. An airplane squadron consists of eighteen machines and 154 men. Eighteen of these men are com-

missioned pilots.   The rest are ground officers,
observers, mechanics, cooks, and guards.   It
can readily be calculated that if we had 20,000
planes in service we should have 1,100 squadrons,
for the operation of which more men would be
required than we had in our army when the war
began.   As a matter of fact, in the first year we
produced fliers four times as fast as we produced
motors.   In the middle of June, 1918, we had in
our service 9,000 flying officers of whom about
1,500 were abroad, most of them completing
their training in French and English schools.
We had in our service some 5,000 machines, the
greatest number of which were training-planes.
By the middle of July the War Department announced that we had built 733 bombing-planes,
of which 425 had been sent abroad.   Most of
these were of a type known as the De Haviland
4, and as in practice they were not proving
entirely satisfactory, orders were given late in
July to build no more, but to construct a later
and better type known as the De Haviland 9.
Meantime orders had been given to scrap a
large number of Bristol fighting-planes which had
been completed.   It was found that the Liberty

motor was too powerful for them, and even had motors been at hand the type had become out of date, so rapidly are the improvements made by those who are actually developing planes under the trying conditions of battle. The needed instruments, such as altimeters and compasses, were not at this time forthcoming in the numbers needed even for training purposes.

At the beginning of the war we had few skilled aviators in the country, and they had to be utilized as instructors. The corps of instructors was enlarged by a large number of foreign flying officers who were sent overseas to our fields to teach our men. That we were able to increase so rapidly our possible flying personnel was due to the energy of the War Department in providing fields and schools, to the patriotism of thousands of young Americans who volunteered for this dangerous service, and to the co-operation of the colleges and universities of the country. These last turned their technical departments over to the government service, and in many of them ground schools were founded, where the embryo fliers could be instructed in the mechanics of motors and in the construction of planes before going to the flying-fields for training in the air. Since the summer of 1917 there has been a steady stream of young men passing through these schools to the flying-fields. So great has their number been that when the airplane production was delayed not enough machines could be had in which to teach them all to fly. Hundreds were sent abroad to take their training in the schools of our allies. The war was a year old before even the training-planes were coming from our factories in numbers sufficient for our needs.

Not only did we have to provide training for our aviators, but schools had to be established to fit men for many phases of the work of the air service. At the factories and in the fields instruction was provided for mechanics, photographers, balloonists, engineers, armorers, and supply and administration officers. The organization of so great a personnel in so short a time has been a work well done.

The work of our aeronautical department has been gaining in momentum. To realize that it is at last under way effectively one has only to visit Long Island. Not a day passes but from early morning to night one can hear the drum of engines high in the air. The planes fly overhead by the scores, some singly, some in battle formation. Often one sees lone aviators practising acrobatics, looping and spiralling, shooting toward earth in the nose-dive or tail-spin, in hair-raising fashion. The skill with which they perform these evolutions gives evidence of their training. In fields all over the country this same dangerous work is being done by an army of as fine young men as have ever taken to the air. To scores of them the training has ended in death, and they have given themselves to the cause of liberty and justice as truly as though they died in battle. The first Americans to die in battle were aviators, and daily the list grows longer with the names of those gallant young souls who have made the supreme sacrifice.

Our aircraft programme will succeed, if somewhat tardily. The invention of the Liberty motor, a good motor which could be made rapidly in large numbers, was an achievement. The trouble was that it was too much advertised and so much expected of it that other matters of equal importance were neglected. One wonders why it was advertised at all. The Germans never knew of the tanks until the tanks were rolling toward them over the Flanders fields, spitting fire. By the vaunting of the motor's virtues and the announcement that it alone would be used on our airplanes, capable inventors were discouraged from efforts in improving engines. We should have had aviation experts in charge of the programme from the beginning, and we did not. More work and fewer optimistic statements on the part of the War Department would have brought efficiency out of confusion much sooner than it really came.

This practically sums up the situation. What has been said is corroborated in the report made public on August 22 by the Senate's investigating committee. This committee found that a substantial part of the original appropriation of $640,000,000 had been wasted. It declared that of the planes sent abroad but 67 De Haviland 4's had reached the front by August 1, and that these were good only for day bombing and observation; that at the same date we had not at the front a single American-made chasse (or plane of attack) or heavy bombing-plane. It found that $6,500,000 was wasted on Bristol planes, as these had to be scrapped, after several lives had been lost in trials. It found that, though 3,000 fast fighting Spads were ordered in September, 1917, this order was cancelled because they could not be adapted to the Liberty motor. It found that, though facilities were ready to build the Caproni bombing-machine in the fall of 1917, only one experimental plane had been completed. While commending the Liberty motor for certain purposes, the committee declared that it was too heavy and too powerful for the lighter types of planes, and that we should have manufactured the best types of foreign motors contemporaneously with its development, instead of which we subordinated all the other phases of the aircraft programme to its perfection and production.

A few days after the Senate committee's report was made public Secretary of War Baker again acted to correct the trouble. He ap-

pointed Mr. Ryan, second assistant secretary of
war, with full charge of all our activities in the
air. Mr. Ryan not only was made responsible
for the production of aircraft, but for operation
of the department of military aeronautics, for
the purpose of co-ordinating both of these
branches of the work. By the same order
Benedict C. Crowell, first assistant secretary,
was placed in charge of the munitions programme, succeeding Mr. Stettinius, who was
then abroad as a special representative of the
department.

The placing of a man of Mr. Ryan's abilities
at the head of our air programme should prove
beneficial. After he became head of the production board marked changes for the better
were noticed. Engines and planes of the best
types were ordered, and our real programme
was put under way. A year late, but still next
year we should prove a power in the combat
in the air.

CHAPTER VII

NAVAL PREPARATION

IN considering the problems faced by America in her preparation for war there has been, at times, a tendency to compare the work of the Navy Department with that of the War Department. Such comparison is unfair. Our navy, at the outbreak of the war, was a finely organized machine, ready for instant action. Our army was so small that it hardly sufficed for police work. Under the theory that the sea protected us from foreign aggression, the navy was always considered our first line of defense, and had been treated with fair generosity by Congress, while the army was stunted and starved by niggardly appropriations. Nearly a year before the beginning of hostilities Congress more than doubled the customary appropriation for naval purposes, allotting large sums of money for new ship construction, for machine-shops, dry-docks, and ordnance. In the same session the army was practically neglected. When we declared war the expansion of the naval force was already under way. Since then the personnel has been increased nearly seven times. In the same period the War Department has had to increase the personnel of the army more than twenty-five times, and contemplates still greater additions to its force. Both departments faced great tasks. The quietness and efficiency with which the Navy Department has been doing its work has merited the highest praise.

The navy was ready. Even before war had been officially declared our sailors were in action from the decks of armed merchantmen, exchanging shots with German submarines. In such an engagement, in the sinking of the *Aztec* on April 1, the first of our fighting men lost his life in service. When war seemed inevitable, Admiral William S. Sims was hurried abroad to get in touch with the British and French admiralties and make arrangements for our entrance into the conflict. When war was begun every available ship was manned and prepared for action. The navy worked quickly and silently. On May 4, in less than a month after hostilities began, we learned that our first flotilla of destroyers had reached a British port, and with added gratification we heard how the British commander, asking when the boats would be ready for action, received the reply: "We are ready now." War-ship followed war-ship. By the close of the year we had in service in European waters 35,000 officers and men, more than one-half the navy's total strength on April 6. One destroyer detachment in the first six months steamed 1,000,000 miles, was 3,600 days at sea, attacked 81 submarines, and escorted 717 merchant vessels safely to port. The first of our armed forces to reach France were naval aviators, who landed on June 8. From the first our navy has made a record for efficiency and daring of which every American has reason to be proud. Working with the fleets of our allies, it has battled with the submarines so successfully as to lessen greatly the menace of the undersea pirates; it has so guarded the ocean lanes that we have landed in France more than a million and a half of men, with a loss of life almost negligible, and have kept moving a steady stream of supply-ships in comparative safety. Under the direction of able men the splendid traditions of our navy have been upheld.

The man directly responsible for these operations at sea is the secretary, Mr. Josephus Daniels. Few men in public life in the past decade have been subject to so much criticism as Mr. Daniels. When, in 1913, he left the editorial desk in his North Carolina newspaper office to join the cabinet, he had little knowledge of naval affairs. He somewhat jarred the sensibilities of both the rank and file of the navy, accustomed to long-established methods of operation and discipline, by instituting a series of reforms. The impression got abroad that he regarded the navy as not so much a fighting-machine as a school for young men. In common with most men in public life he had a hobby, democracy, and he rode it with vigor. His early actions in reform have been described as "amiable floundering." But Mr. Daniels was willing to learn and to listen to able professional advisers, whom he trusted. Many of his reforms proved excellent, even to the minds of those who at first opposed them. Others which were found inadvisable he quietly abandoned. Increased efficiency has come from his fight against the use of alcoholic liquors among the rank and file. The navy has never been an aristocratic institution, but it was formerly impossible for an enlisted man to win an officer's commission. For the responsibilities attending the command of a ship, men had to be trained carefully. The government provides this education at the Naval Academy. The Annapolis cadets come from every part of the country, and every walk of life under carefully laid down rules. Through the initiative of Mr. Daniels the law has been so changed as to allow each year the appointment to Annapolis of 100 enlisted men under the age of twenty. Such a system, while in no way lessening the qualifications required for a commission, certainly gives encouragement to hundreds of ambitious young men who could in no other way find the road open to the quarter-deck. Under the old methods promotions in the commissioned corps were made by seniority. An officer was sure of his promotion even though his attainments and work were mediocre. Mr. Daniels secured the passage of a law by which the promotion of officers above the rank of lieutenant-commander is made by selection. While this does offer an opportunity for favoritism, it allows the placing in posts of responsibility younger, and often abler, men than could be obtained by the seniority principle. There have been times when the secretary's amiable ways and ideas seemed to tend to upset discipline, that necessity in all fighting-machines, but since we entered the war we have heard nothing of these things. He has gathered around him able advisers. Competent men have been placed at the heads of bureaus, and able men in command of our fleets. From the beginning a great work has been carried on efficiently and without friction.

At the outbreak of the war in Europe the American Navy ranked third. Great Britain led with a tonnage of 2,500,000; Germany second, with 951,713 tons; the United States third, with 774,353. In the previous decade we had fallen from second place, a fact not due to the present naval administration but to the failure of an earlier Congress to provide money with which to lay down new vessels. In that decade

the general board of the navy had recom-
mended the construction of 326 new ships of
all classes. Congress granted but 153. From
the beginning of the World War the Navy Department worked consistently to secure a large
increase in the naval establishment, but for the
first two years we find no marked addition to
the appropriations. In 1916 the growing strain
in our relations with Germany did arouse
Congress to action, and legislation was passed
looking to our future needs, both as to ships
and personnel. By the act of August 29, of
that year, the appropriation for the previous
year was more than doubled, and provision
was made for the beginning of a great construction programme, to be carried over three years.
Besides the new ships, the programme provided
for an increase in personnel, a greater aeronautical equipment, new dry-docks, new armor-
plate and projectile plants, new shops, enlarged
navy-yards, instruction camps, and an increase
in reserve supplies of all kinds. For new ships
the programme contemplated the earliest possible construction of ten battleships, six battle
cruisers, ten scout cruisers, fifty destroyers, nine

fleet submarines, fifty-eight coast submarines, and a number of repair and supply vessels. Approximately, a half billion of dollars was needed to complete the construction. Scenting danger in the break in our diplomatic relations with Germany, the Sixty-fourth Congress before its adjournment in the following March passed a still greater appropriation bill for the navy, and the next Congress, in special session, following the declaration of war, enacted two deficiency bills.

The appropriations for the navy for the fiscal year 1917–18 and including the special appropriation of 1916 were as follows:

Act of August 29, 1916...............	$312,888,060.25
Act of March 4, 1917................	516,491,802.08
Act of June 5, 1917.................	514,805,033.87
Act of October 6, 1917..............	561,436,023.50
Total........................	$1,905,620,919.70

For the fiscal year ending July 1, 1919, the present Congress has appropriated $1,616,550,-360 for naval purposes. The sum of these appropriations exceeds the total expenditures in our navy from 1794 to 1916.

When we went to war our navy numbered in service fifteen dreadnaughts, twenty pre-dreadnaughts, ten armored cruisers, twenty-five light cruisers, seven monitors, seventy-four destroyers, nineteen torpedo-boats, and sixty-six submarines. A number of these vessels were out of date. The foresight of the department, in inaugurating the three-year programme seven months before, allowed a rapid and powerful increase in our forces. Within a year many vessels of all classes were added to the navy. How the new construction has proceeded, and details as to the vessels launched or laid down, have not, of course, been announced. In the fall of 1916 there were on the ways six battleships in various stages of construction. Of these only the launching of the *Arizona* has been made public. There were also on the ways at that time ten destroyers and thirty-four submarines, besides several supply-ships. The three-year programme called for the construction, in 1917, of four battleships, four fast battle cruisers, four scout cruisers, twenty destroyers, thirty-one coast-defense submarines, and several supply-ships. When war was declared a large number of additional destroyers were at once ordered, and every available yard set to work on them. Since then the progress of such work has not been made public. Mr. Daniels has stated that within a year the vessels in service have been increased from some 300 to over 1,000, and that we had laid down more destroyers than were to be found in any two combined navies before 1914. It must be remembered, however, that among that thousand vessels are many armed yachts and small submarine chasers which have no value other than for scouting.

The department has officially stated that on April 1, 1917, there were building or authorized for the navy 123 vessels, as follows:

Battleships	15
Battle-cruisers	6
Scout-cruisers	7
Destroyers	27
Submarines	61
Fuel-ships	2
Supply-ship	1
Transport	1
Gunboat	1
Hospital-ship	1
Ammunition-ship	1

It has announced, further, that since that date contracts have been placed for 949 vessels of all kinds, including 100 submarine-chasers for the navies of our allies.

The work thrown on the department by the building programme has been very great, but it has been carried on rapidly and well. At first we lacked yards, ways, shops, and dry-docks. Consideration had to be given also to the pressing needs of the merchant marine, and the programme so carried out as to allow a coincident increase of both the naval and merchant services. These handicaps have been overcome and very rapid construction accomplished, particularly in the matter of torpedo-boat destroyers, so urgently needed to hunt the submarine. Formerly it took from one to two years to build a destroyer. Now the feat is accomplished in from three to five months. Seventeen and a half days after the laying of her keel, the *Ward* was launched at Mare Island, 84 per cent completed. On July 4 sixteen new destroyers slipped from the ways in various parts of the country. To attain this speed in construction the same system of standardization and fabrication as is used for the merchant marine is followed largely. A notable example of the way in which the work is done is to be found at the Ford works at Detroit. Here a fast steel submarine chaser, 200 feet long, is built on a track. The keel is laid, the frame set, the plates riveted on in successive operations as the vessel rolls through the shops, and in an incredibly short time it slips into the river more than 80 per cent completed. The plans for these vessels—eagles, as they are called— were not finished until January. In June the first was launched, and since then the navy has had an almost daily accession of fast and capable little fighters.

To man the greatly increased number of naval vessels demanded an enlargement of the personnel of the force. On April 6, 1917, there were in the navy 69,046 officers and men, and in the Marine Corps 13,692. On July 23 the department announced that the personnel numbered 503,792 officers and men—in the regular navy, 219,158; in the Marine Corps, 58,463; in the Naval Reserve, 219,566; in the Coast Guard, 6,605.

When it authorized the three-year building programme Congress foresaw that more men would be needed for the ships, and in the same act authorized an increase in the regular personnel, and gave the President power to augment the force further in case of emergency. The same legislation formed the United States Naval Reserve. This force is divided into six classes, with varying qualifications laid down for admission, and varying rules as to terms of service. The necessity of war, however, has required that the whole force be treated as one, and as a part of the regular naval service. The men serve in the fighting ships, in the transports and supply-vessels, wherever they are needed. All of this great force has been secured by voluntary enlistment. The selective-service law operates only to furnish men to the army. For the service on the sea young Americans have been offering themselves as fast as they can be equipped and trained. The beginning of the war found the navy some 20,000 men short of its authorized strength, and there were enrolled in the Naval Reserve not more than 10,000. It was necessary to carry on a wide campaign to secure the much-needed men. The nation had to be educated to the needs of its navy. The Navy Publicity Bureau flooded the country with posters and patriotic appeals; meetings were held everywhere to stimulate interest, and the recruiting-stations sent out travelling parties to the remotest districts. Under the stimulus of this campaign the recruiting increased rapidly. To-day the country realizes that it is at war, to a degree that it did not realize a year ago, and little difficulty has been experienced in keeping up a steady flow of splendid young men into our sea service. Every outstanding German outrage has been followed by a rush of volunteers, those who would not wait the operation of the selective-service law to do their bit in fighting the menace of the Hun. Successive legislation has greatly increased the authorized strength of the regular navy, and the law places no limit on the number that can be enrolled in the reserve. For the same reasons the Marine Corps has been increased from hardly more than 10,000 to nearly 75,000.

The equipment and training of these great

forces has been a mighty task for the department. Old training-camps had to be greatly enlarged and new ones built. The problem faced here was much like that of the army in regard to the cantonments, though the construction has not been on so large a scale. In every case model camps have been formed, and every effort has been made to give the young men in them clean and wholesome surroundings during their apprenticeship. The Commission on Training Camp Activities works here as well as in the army cantonments, and with the co-operation of the Y. M. C. A., the Knights of Columbus, and other patriotic bodies, sees that the men's hours of leisure are filled with clean sport and amusement.

The period of service in the naval camps is brief, extending only over a few months. The men are trained there in the rudiments of seamanship and military practice, and then are passed on to service on the sea. For the more intelligent, schools are provided to develop coxswains, quartermasters, naval aviators, aviation mechanics, radio operators, and hospital-corps men.

An idea of the work of these great naval schools can be had from that at Great Lakes, Ill. When the war broke out it was a permanent station fitted to accommodate 1,500 apprentices. Then the boys of the Middle West poured into it by the thousands. At first they had to be sheltered in tents, but a permanent cantonment was built quickly, and to-day nearly 30,000 young sailors are comfortably housed in thoroughly sanitary quarters. In the first six months of the war 50,000 were passed through the camp to the fighting ships. In all the camps the percentage of sickness has been very small, so carefully have the men been guarded against contagion of all kinds. Every newcomer is quarantined for several weeks before he is allowed to come in contact with the main body of his fellows, and he is carefully examined to make sure that he carries no disease germs.

The work of training men for the navy is more difficult than for the army, for the reason that the operation of ships requires many men thoroughly qualified for highly technical tasks. This has been especially true in the matter of

officers. The merchant marine was so small
at the beginning of the war that it could furnish
to the navy few officers qualified for the duties
of the bridge and engine-room. Fortunately
there were in the country thousands of young
men who had had experience in operating small
boats of all kinds, and others whose training at
our technical schools had given a sound basis
for education in the special branches of naval
work. They went to the classes at the Naval
Academy and to officers' schools in the camps,
and in a year of intensive training fitted themselves for commissions in the reserve and for
service at sea. Certain vessels have been used
as schools in gunnery and engineering, and
through them hundreds of young men have
been passing to active duty on our war-ships,
and as armed guards on our merchantmen.
The task of arming our merchantmen has
added greatly to the work of the department.
Before we had declared war we were arming
our merchant ships as a defense against the
submarine, and short though the navy was in
men, thousands of gunners and hundreds of
guns had to be provided for this new service.

A special armed guard division of the navy was formed, and its work has been steadily increased by the output of new vessels, which must have this protection.

Another division that has seen a tremendous increase in personnel and equipment is the Naval Aviation Corps. A year ago this department of our naval work was not greatly developed. At the outbreak of the European War it was, in fact, but little developed in any other navy. The flying-boat, however, early proved its value, not only for scouting purposes but as a weapon against the submarine. As has been said, the first of our armed forces to land in France were naval aviators. Since that time this branch of the service has been greatly augmented. The flying sections of the regular navy, Marine and Reserve Corps now number more than 30,000 men, including flying officers, mechanics, and others. One great plant for the construction of hydroairplanes has been built, and it is turning out machines rapidly.

The foregoing facts give some idea of the vast work entailed on the Navy Department by the war. That the great increase in fighting ships,

in personnel and supplies has been secured so
rapidly and smoothly speaks well for the officers who have had charge of the task. First of
these is Admiral William S. Benson, Chief of
Naval Operations. He is responsible for the
operation of the fleet and for its preparation for
battle; he has to co-ordinate every phase of
naval work so as to secure the greatest effective-
ness against the enemy. We have legally no
general staff in the navy. The Chief of Operations and the heads of the various bureaus,
meeting with the secretary, constitute a war
council, which can act quickly on any important
question that arises. The country has been
fortunate to have, in these trying times, able
men at the head of these important naval bureaus. They had a magnificent machine ready
for war, and steadily they have increased its
power and efficiency. The one thought of these
men, long trained in the high traditions of the
navy, is the good of the service, and the good of
the service is the good of the country.

CHAPTER VIII

OUR NAVY IN ACTION

OUR allies were hard pressed when we joined them in the war on Germany. The collapse of Russia had freed great German armies for service in the west instead of the east. The unrestricted submarine warfare was in the heyday of its success, and the steadily declining merchant tonnage was threatening disaster to Great Britain. Our own ship-building programme was being delayed, and month after month showed more vessels lost than built. Two things had to be done at once: the submarine had to be met in its own haunts, and fighting men sent to the front with all speed and in all possible numbers.

The most troublesome weapon which America had to combat, the cause, in fact, of our entrance into the war, was an American device. As a newspaper man, the writer watched with interest the early development of the submarine. In the fall of 1897, with the assistance of John Holland, he wrote in the New York *Evening Sun* a page giving an account of the then known experiments in underwater navigation, and including prophecies of some naval men of vision as to its future development. Since then volumes have been written on the subject. If he remembers correctly, the first known experiment with a submarine was made in a Spanish harbor some two hundred years ago, and it ended disastrously for the inventor. In our Revolution, Bushnell, an American inventor, contrived a hand-propelled underwater boat, which navigated from Tarrytown to Fort George, Staten Island, and there attempted, unsuccessfully, to blow up a British war-ship with a crude bomb. A keg of powder was carried in the top of the submarine, and it was purposed to attach this to the hull of the warship by means of a screw, cast loose, and let a timed clock explode the bomb. The warship's hull so resisted the turn of the screw that the operator had to abandon the enterprise, but he got safely home. Robert Fulton devised a submarine of much the same type, and offered it to Napoleon for service against the fleets of England. In the Civil War, a submarine of considerable size which had been devised by a Confederate officer went down with all on board, in Charleston harbor, while attempting to attack a Federal cruiser. All these boats submerged by taking on water-ballast, and the great problem of the inventors was to find means of propulsion. Holland, in his experiments with the boats which he built in the '80's, had a small gas-engine, and this used up the air so rapidly that he could not stay submerged for any time. He devised a new method of submerging by means of horizontal rudders, and worked out devices to make for safety and accuracy in navigation. The development of the storage-battery as a means of storing electric energy solved the difficulty of power. In 1892 he secured an order from the Navy Department to build a submarine torpedo-boat, the *Plunger*. It was to travel on the surface by steam and under water by electric power. This craft was begun but never finished. About this time a French inventor was working on a submarine with success. With the help of private enterprise Holland, in the fall of 1897, laid the keel of another submarine, called the *Holland*, at Nixon's ship-yard at Elizabethport, N. J. It was launched in March of the next year, and the *Evening Sun* of that date published a page account of the vessel, but the event was regarded as of so little importance as to be almost disregarded by the other papers. Not many weeks later the tiny vessel was navigating under the waters of New York harbor, her performances being watched with wondering eyes by naval men. But the Navy Department did not take kindly to the submarine. The craft was too revolutionary, the battleship was the pet of the construction department, and it gave little encouragement to Holland or to the other men who now set about perfecting this manner of craft. A few boats were ordered, but for years we lagged behind other nations in the development of the type. Great Britain, Germany, and France were less slow in seizing on the new naval weapon, and how Germany has used it the world knows to its sorrow.

The fleets of Great Britain drove the German

Navy from the sea almost the day war was declared. Only in her submarines had Germany an effective naval weapon, and these proved almost powerless to accomplish anything against the vigilant British men-of-war. To the astonishment of civilized peoples, they were turned against helpless merchantmen, and began their career of murder. An unarmed ship was at their mercy. From an armed ship they could always seek safety in the depths. To destroy the submarine became the perplexing problem of the allied navies. Numerous methods were followed, but it was found that the most effective was a careful patrol by armed vessels of the infested sea areas. Many small, fast, armed motor-boats were built, and for a while did good work, but the ever-increasing size of the pirate craft and their heavier armament soon made them more than a match for the lightly armed chaser. Now the main reliance is placed on fast destroyers and hydroairplanes.

Our Navy Department early realized the danger of the submarine, and long before we entered the war it was devising means to meet it, should the necessity arise. An important step in the work of preparedness was the formation of the Naval Consulting Board, a body of men skilled in every branch of science, who placed their services at the government's disposal. It was formed in 1915, with Thomas A. Edison at its head, and has been working ever since at the problems of offense and defense in naval warfare. Naturally, a flood of suggestions for dealing with the submarines has been submitted to it, and the great part of them have not proved of value. Since we went to war the National Research Council, another scientific body connected with the Council of National Defense, has been working over the same problem. The results of the labors of these two bodies have not been made public, but it is known that they, in conjunction with similar bodies in the service of our allies, have perfected some very effective devices for locating and destroying the submarine. One of them, the depth-bomb, which dropped from a vessel or hydroairplane explodes at a given depth, destroying any craft within a considerable area, has proved the destruction of many of the pirates.

The first duty of the navy when war was

declared was to attack the submarine, and it did so with great promptness. In less than a month our first flotilla of destroyers had arrived on the other side of the Atlantic and was engaged in active operations against the Germans. The patrol of this side of the sea was taken over by our vessels, releasing for service in the more infested waters a number of our allies' ships. The first flotilla was followed by other squadrons, and to-day thousands of our seamen are working with their fellows of England and France making the seas safe for transport of all kinds. That the co-operation of the allied navies has been attended with marked success is evidenced by the gradual but steady decline in the number of ships torpedoed, and by the continuing increase in the number of hostile U-boats sunk. The exact figures as to the destruction of these U-boats have never been made public, but we have the assurance of the British Government that, because of the strengthened patrol and improved offensive methods, their destruction since the beginning of the year 1918 has exceeded their replacement.

The second great operation of our navy was to get our military forces overseas. Germany has belittled America as a foe because she did not believe it possible for us to send a force of any importance so great a distance, especially through waters infested by her U-boats. She learned her mistake when, in June, our gallant marines at Château-Thierry helped to stop her rush toward Paris. Had she doubts then, she must have been convinced that we really had an army at the Marne when thousands of our soldiers threw themselves upon her armies and helped to drive them from the Château-Thierry salient. A million and a half men moved in a year and a half to France, and the prospect of the number doubled within a year must make her wonder.

The forces we could send to France in the early months were only small. Aside from our Regular Army, we had not the men then ready. But France was calling for even the moral support of a small force. Ships for transports were lacking. Almost at the moment war was declared we had seized in our ports 118 interned enemy vessels, but these had been so badly damaged by their crews as not to be ready for service at that time. Such suitable vessels as could be had from our small merchant marine and from our allies were gathered together in various harbors, and about the middle of June, in one great convoy, they set forth over the Atlantic carrying the first contingents of our Regular Army and a vast quantity of supplies. The Germans had been apprised of their coming and a flotilla of submarines was lying in wait. They attacked the convoy off the French coast, but the vigilance of our destroyers and the accuracy of their fire drove off the U-boats, at least one of which, it is believed, was sent to the bottom. On June 25 the entire fleet arrived safely in a French harbor. Not a life was lost in this expedition. Since that time a steady movement of transports and supply-ships has kept going and coming over the seas, and thanks to the navy's vigilance the loss of life as compared with the great number of troops carried has been almost negligible. In a year but two transports were lost. The *Antilles* was sunk while returning from France. The *Tuscania*, a British vessel carrying our soldiers, was sent to the bottom and several hundred lives were lost. The *Finland* was torpedoed, but reached a British port under her own steam.

The German Government calculated that the lack of vessels and the attacks of the submarines would make a great movement of American troops impossible. The navy has rendered the submarine ineffective. The difficulty over the ship shortage has been solved by the co-operation of the navy and the shipping board. At the end of six months all the German vessels which we seized had been repaired and were in the government service. But to carry the men has not been the only problem. With them a steady supply of food and ordnance of all kinds has to be kept moving and protected, and the handling of so many vessels and the vast quantities of stores necessitated practically the reconstruction of a French port and a great increase in its docking facilities.

The movement of our troops abroad in 1917 was not great. Hardly more than 300,000 men were sent over. Then in the late winter our National Guard and National Army were ready to start to the front. By this time the submarine had been curbed and many new vessels were coming from our ways, though we had still to rely largely on our allies, and particularly on Great Britain, for transports. The massing of heavy German armies in the west, threatening a desperate attack on the allied line, caused France and Great Britain to send us an urgent appeal for all possible fighting men, and the movement of troops in the spring and summer was accelerated to a degree that a year ago would have seemed incredible. In the month of June, 276,370 soldiers were carried over, and in July more than 300,000. To that time the total loss of life in the perilous movement had been less than 300. In the meanwhile the work of the allied navies against the submarines was telling, as was shown by the steadily decreasing loss of tonnage. The total loss for June was 81,905 gross tons less than in May. The sinkings in July were one-half those of the same month last year.

The navy has not only had to protect the transports, but in many cases it has had to man them. The transport service is really in charge of a division of the War Department, which has branches in all our great ports, and supervises the operation of the vessels. The navy's main task is that of policing the seas, but it has also to furnish armed guards to all vessels that pass through the danger zone. There has been difficulty in finding civilian crews to man the great number of new merchantmen sailing under our flag, and in such cases the army and the shipping board have had to call on the navy for assistance, and crews have been supplied. For this work the Naval Reserve force has proved of special value, as it contains many men who have seen service in the merchant marine.

In writing of the mobilization of our naval forces for war, it is fitting that mention should be made of that gallant corps, our soldiers of the sea, who have been acquitting themselves so bravely on the soil of France. The motto of the marine corps is *Semper Fidelis*. To the popular mind it is "The First to Fight." In every war in which America has engaged, the marines have conducted themselves gallantly, and never have they failed to live up to the high traditions of their service. Under the old theory the marines were the police of the ship, and as a consequence did not enjoy high favor with the jackies. In battle they fought with small arms and were of special value in landing-parties. Before this war their service was always in small units. To-day they are fighting in divisions as a part of our army.

The history of the corps intertwines with that of both army and navy. Marines fought under John Paul Jones on the *Ranger* and the *Bon Homme Richard*. In the war with Tripoli, in 1803, they played a conspicuous part, and they had a hand in the War of 1812, both on sea and land. In the Mexican War a body of marines were the first of our forces to enter the city of Mexico. There is hardly a year in American history when our marines have not been on dangerous duty somewhere in the world keeping order and upholding the honor of the flag. They made the first landing in Cuba in 1898, and fought their way to Pekin with the allied troops in the Boxer campaign. When the present war came the corps was ready as always, trained to the minute and equipped to the last button, and a brigade of them formed part of our first forces to land in France.

The strength of the corps has usually been kept about one-fourth that of the navy personnel. On April 6, 1917, it numbered 13,692 officers and men, and the President was authorized to increase its war strength to 17,400, which was rapidly done. Successive legislation, designed to make its growth keep pace with that of our other forces, has raised its numbers to nearly 75,000. All these have been volunteers, and a finer lot of men would be hard to find. The physical qualifications for the service have always been very high, and even under the necessity of obtaining thousands of recruits these standards have been but little relaxed. The romance of the service by sea and land "from the shores of Tripoli to the halls of Montezuma," has had a wide appeal among the young men of the country. The corps offers opportunities for rapid advancement, and hundreds of highly educated men have gone into its ranks with the purpose of working their way up to commissions. The needs of our growing navy in the past twenty years have made it necessary that all the trained Annapolis graduates be put into the line. For a time many of the marine corps officers were appointed from civil life, but to-day it secures them almost entirely from its own ranks. It has become a great military school in which every man is made to feel the honor of the service and is taught the obligation of upholding its splendid record. It has become a body of fighting men in physique and training the equal of any in the world.

The rapid expansion of the corps in the past year has been splendidly accomplished. Recruits go to the great camps at Paris Island, S. C., or Mare Island, Cal. Here they undergo fourteen weeks of intensive training. Cleanliness of person, implicit obedience, precision in drill and accurate shooting are absolute requirements. The men who are chosen for overseas duty are sent to complete their training at Quantico, Va. This is one of the model war-schools of the country. Here actual fighting conditions have been simulated to a greater degree than in any other of our cantonments. The barracks are the acme of cleanliness and healthful conditions. A training-ground hundreds of acres in extent gives room for artillery and rifle ranges, and a great trench system, with wire entanglements and dugouts. From these trenches in their training the men have been sent out into No Man's Land behind a real barrage of artillery-fire. Training under such conditions is the nearest thing to actual fighting that our men see on this side of the water.

All of our navy camps are splendidly located and managed. Their situation near large bodies of water adds much to their health. The writer has visited several of them and found them alike in their standards of health and comfort. The large station for the reserve at Pelham Bay Park on Long Island Sound is an excellent example of them. The writer was fortunate enough to have a sailor friend there who guided him from the main gate through all the working parts of this big school for seamen. Close by the gate are the huts of the Y. M. C. A. and the Knights of Columbus, where, it being noon, scores of young sailors were found writing, reading, and amusing themselves with music and games. To my guide's inquiry as to what I wished to see first, the reply was, "Food," and I was led to the great mess-hall. The kitchen was spotless. We lined up before the affable cooks and received a tin plate with a plentiful helping of excellent beefsteak, carrots, potatoes, and green peas, a cup of coffee and a plate of stewed peaches. These we consumed at the long tables in the mess-hall with the added luxury of the first white bread I had seen in a year. The meal over, we began our tour, going first to the bakery, where thousands of loaves of that delicious white bread were being made. Thence we went to the storerooms and they would have been a model for any first-class hotel. In the enlistment bureau we followed the process that changes a civilian into a seaman. In one room a score of young men still in mufti were filling out their papers; in the next another score were sitting in the clothes they were born in beside the discarded apparel of civil life; in the next a half dozen Apollo Belvideres were being pounded by surgeons and jabbed with needles; in the last there were more, scrambling into clothes again, but now

Mess at the Pelham Bay Naval Station.

"We lined up before the affable cooks and received a tin plate with a plentiful helping . . . which we consumed at the long tables in the mess-hall."

the clothes allotted to them by Uncle Sam. We emerged into the detention-camp. Here the rookies stay three weeks in quarantine, carefully wired off from the rest of the camp. For the better control of any contagion their barracks are divided so that only a small squad is housed in one room. We passed back to the main camp. Here each barrack is occupied by one company. The buildings are light, airy, and scrupulously clean. In them the new sailors get their first taste of sea ways, for they sleep in hammocks. In daytime the hammocks are neatly rolled against the wall beside the canvas bag that contains the owner's equipment; at night they stretched between iron-pipe jack-stays, and if the men feel none of the motion of a ship they have at least a touch of the fo'c'sle.

That afternoon the bay was alive with boats, the crews pulling at their oars under the commands of vociferous petty officers. In the school barracks scores of young aspirants for commissions were poring over text-books and listening to lectures on the technic of the sailor's profession. On the parade-ground, under the eyes of the commandant, six companies from the detention-camp were drilling earnestly in a competition which promised a day's leave from camp for the winning company. On the water, in the schools, on the drill-grounds thousands of white-clad young men were working hard to fit themselves for their country's service. They were men from the colleges and schools, from the factories, shops, and farms. Many of them, perhaps, had little knowledge of the underlying causes of the war. To all of them the vital thing was that their country was in arms against a race of outlaws and willingly and cheerfully they were hardening themselves to do their bit in the whipping of the Hun.

CHAPTER IX

THE FOOD CAMPAIGN

THE fourth great problem which the government has had to solve in its conduct of the war has been that of food. It is an exaggeration to say that food will win the war. Food is but one of the weapons with which the victory will be won. The battle to produce and conserve food is one in which the humblest of us has been able to have a part. It was the campaign for increased production and conservation that first brought to the mass of the people a realization that we were in a war the winning of which demanded personal sacrifice of every American. Before an American soldier had set foot in France we were ploughing new fields and taking stock of our larder.

To reach an understanding of the pressing food problem of to-day one has to consider the situation of the world as to food-supplies before 1914. In the decade before that Europe had been unable to increase the production of the staple food, wheat. Vast as were our resources, America, in the same period, had not increased her power of export to any great degree. Europe had to be fed largely from outside, and for a great part of her wheat depended on the plains of Asia, South America, and Australia. When the war came our present allies were shut off from the Russian and Rumanian fields. It is estimated that in the year 1917 there were in Russia, China, India, and Argentine about four hundred million bushels of exportable wheat, but war and lack of transport made it impossible to get it to our allies. Australia to-day has in her elevators an exportable surplus of nearly two hundred million bushels of wheat, but while a ship is making one round trip between Sydney and Europe she can make three to America. The free movement of crops has long been vital to the life of Europe, and when this movement was hampered by the war, famine was threatened. Making the danger of starvation greater was the fact that millions of men were withdrawn from the farms to serve in the armies and munition-factories. It is estimated that in the countries of our allies the destructive activities of war have withdrawn nearly forty million men from the productive activities of peace. Before the war France had to import 30 per cent of her food. In 1917 her cereal crop was 40 per cent below the pre-war average. Great Britain in peace-times imports 50 per cent of her food. To-day she is getting nearly 44 per cent of her food-supply from America.

The following table gives clear proof of Great Britain's dependence on the sea for life. It gives the average per cent of certain foodstuffs home produced and imported during the years from 1906 to 1913.

	HOME PRODUCED	IMPORTED
Meat..................	59	41
Wheat................	22	88
Barley...............	60	40
Oats..................	80	20
Potatoes..............	97	3
Butter................	35	65
Cheese................	25	75
Apples................	58	42
Corn..................	practically none	—
Fish..................	practically all	—

When, in 1914, the great sources of supply in
Asia were cut off, and the long haul from India,
Australia, and South America made it unfeasi-
ble to secure much food there, our allies and the
neutral countries turned for help to the nearest
markets, our own. The result of this demand,
even before our entrance into the war, was a
rapid rise in the price of all foodstuffs. According to government reports in the five years
previous to June, 1918, there was an average
increase of 66 per cent of the price of all foodstuffs in America. Had we not had recourse to
governmental regulation, that increase would
have been much greater. Wheat which in 1914
was selling around $1 a bushel, in the spring of
1917 rose from $1.44 to $3, and the prices of
all other basic foodstuffs were sky-rocketing in
the same way.

Our entrance into the war found our allies in
great distress as to food-supplies. It found their
own food production steadily declining, and the
submarine, then in the heyday of its successes,
sinking many tons of precious cargoes vital to
their life. We promised them three things,
men, ships, and food. Germany was boasting

that within six months she would by starvation bring Great Britain to her knees. She has not starved Great Britain and she will not because Americans know that the life of Great Britain and France is vital to America's safety; they know that if our allies fail to get food we shall be left to fight alone and that the war will come to our coast. In the field and in the kitchen they have been carrying on a work that is a part of the great offensive to crush the enemy. The moment they entered the war they were told by the government what had to be done, and they have done it willingly. The food campaign has been one of universal service.

In pre-war days Great Britain, France, Italy, and Belgium imported yearly some 750,000,000 bushels of grain and vast quantities of animal and fat products. In the three years before the war the United States exported a yearly average of 120,000,000 bushels of grain (wheat, corn, oats, barley, and rye) and 500,000,000 pounds of animal products and fats. In the year 1917 the Allies' production of cereals had diminished by 525,000,000 bushels, and herds of cattle, sheep, and swine by 30,000,000 animals. The continuation of the war promised an ever-increasing shortage in their supplies. In the fiscal year 1916–17 we exported 400,000,-000 bushels of grain and 1,500,000,000 pounds of animal products and fats. To do this we had reduced our food stocks to the lowest figure, relatively, in our history, and we were killing animals faster than we were raising them. When we joined the Allies in the fight for freedom it ceased to be merely a matter of business to send them food. It became a deep obligation and a work of patriotism. For the year 1917–18 our allies called for 525,000,000 bushels of wheat, their basic ration, and our normal export of wheat had been only 80,000,000 bushels; Canada's normal export was 100,000,000 bushels and it was possible for them to get but little from the more distant markets. This situation left a wide gap to be filled, and the same difficulty presented itself, not with wheat alone but with every other foodstuff. The problem could never have been solved without government supervision and nation-wide co-operation.

Fortunately the government had ready for service Herbert C. Hoover, who, from the outbreak of the war in Europe until our own entrance into it, had been working as the head of the American Commission for Relief in Belgium. In working out the difficult problem of rationing millions of starving Belgians Mr. Hoover became an expert on food-supply and food values. When he went to Washington in the spring of 1917 he had for months no authority for effective action. He could only work informally with the sanction of President Wilson. He organized an office force, composed largely of volunteers, and this force was the nucleus of what subsequently became under the law the United States Food Administration. The first work done was largely that of propaganda. A campaign of education was carried on. The pressing needs of our allies were explained to the people of the country and on them was impressed the absolute necessity of raising more food and of using and wasting less. On August 10 the so-called Lever bill became a law, and under its broad powers the President was enabled to organize the Food and the Fuel Administrations.

As essential to the national security the bill is

designed "to assure an adequate supply and an equal distribution and to facilitate the movement of foods, feeds, fuel, including fuel-oil and natural gas" and of fertilizers and of the machinery and implements used in the production of these necessities.

At his discretion the President is empowered to license all persons engaged in producing, storing, or dealing in these necessities, except that farmers and gardeners, and retailers doing less than $100,000 gross business yearly are exempted. He can require the licensees to make reports for inspection by his agents. If it is found that "the storage charge, commission profit, or practice of any licensee is unjust or unreasonable, or discriminatory and unfair or wasteful," and such practice is not discontinued, the license may be revoked. Without a license the business cannot be continued, under a penalty of fine, or imprisonment, or both.

Hoarding is prohibited, and is made punishable by a fine, or imprisonment, or both.

The use of any foodstuffs, grains or fruits, in the distillation of spirits for beverages is forbidden.

The President is authorized when necessary to the public welfare to requisition storage facilities, and he can take over and operate any factory, packing-house, mine, and pipe-line or other plant used in the production or moving of the necessities named, but in all such cases he must make just compensation to the owners.

He can purchase and provide storage facilities for, and sell at reasonable prices for cash, wheat, flour, meal, beans, and potatoes. In such cases he must pay for these commodities the minimum price, if such minimum price has been fixed under the later provisions of the law.

If he finds that an emergency exists requiring the stimulation of the production of wheat, he can give public notice of what is a reasonable price for wheat in order to insure the producers a reasonable profit. Thereupon the government guarantees every producer of wheat this reasonable price. The law provided that until May 1, 1919, the price should not be fixed at less than $2 per bushel.

The President was further authorized to fix the price of coal and coke, "wherever and whenever sold, either by producer or dealer."

An appropriation of $150,000,000 was made to carry out the provisions of the act. This sum constitutes a revolving fund to be used in the work of purchasing and selling the commodities named.

Immediately on signing the bill the President appointed Mr. Hoover United States Food Administrator, and Mr. Hoover and his associates organized the United States Food Administration.

The problem facing the Food Administration was a difficult one. Production had to be increased and consumption reduced with the least possible disarrangement of the ordinary processes of trade. Opinions as to the best methods varied. High and rising wages with wide-spread employment promised increased consumption. On the other hand, if increased production were obtained by allowing the prices of foodstuffs to rise unrestrained, it was contended that a great burden would be thrown on those least able to pay. It was decided that prices must be regulated and production stimulated and waste eliminated by an appeal to the patriotism of the people. The Food Administration soon became a great business organization, dealing in basic foodstuffs and regulating trade and at the same time conducting a patriotic propaganda.

The President on August 14 authorized the formation of the Food Administration Grain Corporation, with a capital stock of $50,000,000, all held by the government, with a purpose to buy and sell wheat. This stock has since been trebled. A few days later the Grain Corporation opened agencies at all the principal primary grain-markets and began its work of dealing in wheat, at a price of $2.20 per bushel, with certain differentials for locality and grade, fixed by the President. There is nothing in the law that prevents any one from buying or selling at another price, but the government's action acted automatically to hold the price at the fixed figure. It is manifest that nobody would sell wheat at a less figure than the government was ready to give for it, and that no one would buy it at a greater figure than the government would pay for it, as the government was always ready to undersell him afterward. Through its system of licenses, the government has been able to supervise the dealings in grain, and has wiped out much of the cost of the movement from producer to consumer by reducing the profits of the middlemen. After its purchase of wheat it sells to the miller with only a very small charge for overhead expenses of operation. It has eliminated speculation and extortionate charges by middlemen. It has another lever of control by its purchases of all foodstuffs for our allies abroad and the supervision of the exports to neutrals. The sales to the Allies are made at price-levels prevailing here, so that the producer has no better market than that at home. To prevent the home wheat-market from being undersold by imports, the President has power to raise the tariff to a protective point.

The result of the first year of the operations in wheat has been that the consumer has been paying less per barrel for flour, while the farmer's profit has increased more than 60 cents a bushel for wheat, which is equivalent to about $3 for a barrel of flour. In May, 1917, flour was selling at Minneapolis for $16.75 a barrel. A year later the price had gone down to $9.80. In peace-times, of the price of a pound of bread the farmer took an average of less than 30 per cent, the miller about 7 per cent and the baker about two-thirds. In the present year the farmer receives approximately 45 per cent, the baker 49 per cent, and the miller 6 per cent. By such processes has the planting of wheat been stimulated and the price of flour, which threatened to go over $20 a barrel, been kept down.

To regulate the prices of all staple commodities the Food Administration exercised its right to call on all wholesale dealers to take out licenses. It further asked their co-operation in carrying out the provisions of the law and in the great majority of cases this has been given heartily. An arrangement with the sugar-refiners was early effected, by which they agreed to refine on a net profit margin, between the cost of their material and the selling price of their product, of 1.3 cents per pound, after deducting trade discounts. By this agreement the price of sugar was prevented from sky-rocketing to $50 a barrel. Like results were obtained from other agreements between the administration and the dealers. By its power to

call for frequent reports from the businesses
involved, the administration has been able to
scrutinize the charges and profits made. Where
it has found these unfair or objectionable practices indulged in, it has issued orders for immediate correction. When its orders have not
been carried out, it has revoked the licenses of
the offenders.

But while the administration has wide powers
of control over the large dealers, its powers of
regulation of the small retailers are more limited. In Germany the final selling price of an
article is fixed by law, but the German Government, with its autocratic power, can compel production, no matter how dissatisfied the producer
may be with his return. Under our system of
government there was no power to compel a
farmer to raise crops. It was necessary to insure him a just return for his labor, and then,
to keep down the ultimate price of his products,
the system established aimed to eliminate the
middlemen's profits as far as possible and to
reduce waste. The Food Administration has no
power to license retail dealers doing a gross
business of less than $100,000 a year and 95

per cent of those in the country are in this class. A wide campaign was carried on to secure the co-operation of these unlicensed dealers. With the help of travelling salesmen who were made special representatives of the government, more than 250,000 of the 350,000 small retail grocers of the country enrolled as members of the Food Administration. They signed pledges to give their customers the benefit of fair and moderate prices, which they could do because the government controlled the prices until the products reached their stores. Every retailer who joins the Food Administration receives a certificate, which every customer in his store can see. Any retailer who does not live up to the pledge or who charges unfair prices is likely to receive no more supplies from the wholesale dealers, for they are forbidden to sell to violators of the regulations.

By all these means the prices of staple foodstuffs have been held within reasonable bounds, but coincident with this work it was necessary to carry on a campaign of conservation. The Food Administration became a great department of our government, spreading its power into the

remotest sections of our country. In every
state there is a federal food administrator,
and under him in nearly every county a subordinate food official. These men are charged
with the enforcement of the law, and have, besides, to conduct a campaign of education, to
encourage production and conservation. The
work has been carried on largely by patriotic
volunteers. The food-saving movement quickly
assumed wide proportions. The co-operation of
the people was asked in limiting their consumption and using those foods of which we have
abundance in place of those of which there was
a scarcity, in order that we might send everything needed to our soldiers overseas, and to
those who were fighting with us. The people
responded willingly. Within a year after the
administration began its work, more than
12,000,000 persons signed cards pledging themselves to adhere to the rules laid down in the
conservation programme, as issued from time
to time by the government. These pledges
called for certain wheatless and meatless days
every week, and for an endeavor to prevent
waste and to save sugar and fats.

To carry out successfully so great a campaign of education has required an army of workers. Through the churches, women's clubs, fraternal lodges, and commercial travellers' organizations the administration obtained thousands of volunteers. Sixty thousand commercial travellers have enrolled as special representatives, and their reports on conditions as they find them on their trips about the country have proved exceedingly valuable. Through the efforts of these various organizations fully half the people of the United States have been reached personally and appealed to to do their bit in raising food and in saving it. An important element in the saving of food has been the spreading of the knowledge of food values, the teaching of economical methods of cooking, and the use of substitutes having equal nutritious value. Along these lines the Home Economics Division works. This division has its representatives in every State, and it works in close co-operation with the county representatives of the Women's Council of National Defense, through whom it keeps in touch with hundreds of thousands of housekeepers. Under its direction courses in household economics have been established in 485 colleges and 236 normal schools, from which women trained in food uses and values have gone into field-work to spread their knowledge. Through the work of the Food Administration, with the co-operation of the vast majority of the people, the battle for food is being won.

CHAPTER X

HELPING OUR ALLIES

WHEAT is the basic ration of all civilized nations. It forms 39 per cent of the total diet in the United States, 67 per cent of the diet of France, and of Italy's a still larger percentage. America uses in its ration a great deal of corn, but our allies are not accustomed to this food. They have but few mills where it can be ground and the meal deteriorates so rapidly as to make it not good for export. In 1917, as we have seen, our allies were calling on us and on Canada for more than twice the amount of wheat that was in normal times available for export. They had reduced their pre-war consumption of wheat more than 25 per cent; of sugar, fats, and oils 50 per cent. Our own 1917 wheat-crop was 150,000,000 bushels short of the average of 800,000,000, and by March, 1918, there was left in the country only enough for the normal needs of the people. The entire surplus had been exported.

To ship more abroad we had to save. The President, on January 18, issued a proclamation urging greater efforts to save food, especially wheat. The Food Administration acted to curtail the use of wheat. It ordered millers to make more flour from a given weight of grain by using 4 per cent more of the berry than had been the custom. It issued orders limiting wholesale dealers in cereals to 70 per cent of the flour purchases in the corresponding periods of 1917, and compelled them to sell wheat-flour only to retailers who bought a corresponding amount of other cereals. The retailers were required to sell flour only to customers who bought equal quantities of other cereals. All manufacturers of macaroni, crackers, breakfast foods, pastries, etc., were likewise limited to 70 per cent of their purchases of flour in 1917. For the bakers a standard loaf was adopted with regulations as to the quantities of sugar and shortening, and they were required to mix with their wheat-flour 20 per cent of the flour of other grains. Through the bakeries alone a great saving of wheat was effected, since 40 per cent of the country's stock passes through them to the consumer. Further saving was made by the action of more than 200,000 proprietors of hotels and restaurants pledging themselves to restrict the use of wheat in any form until the new harvest was in, and by the action of the householders in substituting breads made of corn-meal and other cereals for wheat bread. These measures were effective. We saved enough wheat to tide over our allies until the harvest of the present year was coming in. On July 28 the Food Administration announced that the crisis was passed and released the hotel and restaurant men from their pledges.

It was impossible for the United States and Canada to send to Europe all the wheat needed there, but with small imports from other countries and by careful regulation and the substitution of other foods, our allies were able to pass safely a crisis that threatened serious consequences. To accomplish this we had to reduce our own consumption of wheat from 42,000,000 bushels a month to 30,000,000 bushels. Answering the appeal of the government, the farmers this year planted a greatly enlarged acreage. With a large crop, with an improvement in our railroad traffic, and an increased merchant marine, it is expected that the problem of getting the needed bread to our allies will not in the future be so difficult as in the past, if the wise regulation continues and the people carry on their sacrifice, which, after all, has proved but a little hardship.

Americans have not had to save wheat alone. Wheat has been the most vital element in the battle for food, but there have been other problems of almost equal importance. The herds of our allies had been greatly reduced, and the dislocation of shipping rendered it difficult for them to get their meat products in the customary quantities from Argentine. It was not feasible to carry sugar from the distant markets, and to make good these deficits of meat and sugar they had to look to us. Even before we entered the war we had been slaughtering our animals to a dangerous degree. To maintain a continuous supply of meat products for ourselves and our allies, it was necessary that the killing of animals be curtailed as far as possible and a steady supply of meat products secured by a reduction of the individual's consumption. This result was obtained through the agency of the Food Administration's rules and propaganda. Meatless days as well as wheatless days were instituted, and as a result without any appreciable diminution of our herds we have been able to send abroad vast quantities of meat products. By a gradual reduction of the sugar ration per person per month we have been able to spare considerable stocks for our friends overseas.

The report of the Food Administration for the fiscal year, July 1, 1917–18, shows clearly what America has accomplished in the matter of helping to feed our allies.

Of meats and fats, including dairy products and vegetable oils, we sent to them and to our expeditionary armies 3,011,100,000 pounds, an increase of 844,600,000 pounds over the previous year.

Of cereals and cereal products, reduced to the terms of cereal bushels, we sent them 340,803,000 bushels, an increase of 80,900,000 bushels. Of these cereals our shipments of wheat were 131,000,000 bushels and of rye 13,900,000 bushels. In addition 10,000,000 bushels of 1917 wheat were then on their way to allied ports. The total shipment of wheat of the 1917 harvest was therefore about 141,000,000 bushels. In 1916–17, when we had a larger crop, we sent abroad 135,100,000 bushels of wheat and 2,300,-000 bushels of rye.

In addition, we sent to neutral countries, dependent on us for food, 10,000,000 bushels of prime foodstuffs, wheat and rye.

The following table shows in what degree our efforts have helped to feed our allies.

COUNTRY	POPULATION	APPROXIMATE NUMBER MEN SUPPORTED BY PRESENT UNITED STATES EXPORTS	PER CENT OF TOTAL POPULATION SUPPORTED BY PRESENT UNITED STATES EXPORTS
United Kingdom..	46,000,000	20,000,000	43.5
France..........	39,000,000	5,500,000	14.1
Italy............	36,000,000	4,000,000	11.1

Mr. Hoover has calculated that, in spite of the fact that the nutritional production of the country for the past fiscal year was more than 7 per cent lower than the average of the three previous years, we exported a nutritional surplus at least 7 per cent greater, showing how the consumption and waste of food was reduced by the efforts of our people.

Besides helping to fill the larders of our allies, America has been feeding the populations of Belgium and the parts of northern France occupied by the Germans. This means that nine millions of people have been depending on us for life. When the German armies had over-run Belgium and northern France, ruthlessly destroying all the sources of life for these unfortunate people, an appeal was made to America, then neutral, for help. The Commission for Relief in Belgium was formed. It was at first operated as a private charity. From the fall of 1914 to the day of our entering the war it had sent to Belgium 2,562,000 tons of clothing and foodstuffs. To carry this it chartered a fleet of some forty steamships. German kultur has not spared these vessels on their errands of mercy. Eighteen of them have been destroyed by submarines or mines. But their work has continued and to-day, flying the flag of the commission, they travel over certain fixed routes under guarantee of the German Government that they will not be molested. '

When we went to war all the American representatives of the commission had to leave Belgium, but the work has since been carried on through different agencies. The commission has established agencies in Washington, New York, London, and Rotterdam, where all purchases are handled. The food is shipped through Holland and is controlled by representatives of the commission up to the Belgium border. Here the Belgium agent of the commission receives it and turns it over to the Belgium National Committee which supervises its distribution. Under a plan formulated before the withdrawal of the American delegates on May 1, 1917, the Spanish and Dutch delegates took charge of the work of guarding the supplies and seeing that they reached the suffering people. Any infractions of the guarantees given by the German Government not to confiscate any domestic or imported foodstuffs, they report to their ministers, who endeavor to have the agreement enforced.

To support this great work, the United States Government advances to the commission $9,000,000 monthly for Belgium and $6,000,000 for northern France. These sums are simply loans to the respective governments. The European expenditures are met from the French and British treasuries, and bring the total up to about $20,000,000 monthly. This sum barely suffices to send to the needy people a life-sustaining ration and much-needed clothing. The basic ration provided is made up of wheat, corn, rice, dried peas and beans, bacon, lard, and condensed milk, and an effort is made to see that 120,000 tons of these foods monthly cross the Dutch border to the stricken regions. Supplementary meals and medicines and supplies for children, the aged and sick, have to be supplied by private funds given to the commission.

The food-conservation campaign has given a great lesson to Americans. Feeding Belgium is not rightly charity. It is rather helping to pay a part of the great debt owing to the gallant little nation which kept faith with the world and delayed the first onrush of the Huns. To the men who are offering their lives for us on the battle-fields of France we owe another great debt. To eat less and save more is an unheroic way of helping the country to fight its battles, but it has been brought home to all Americans that the field and the kitchen are supporting lines of our armies and our allies, and they must not fail them.

CHAPTER XI

THE WAR BUDGET

A FEW years ago it would have seemed incredible that America would ever be called on to spend in one war more money than the government had expended in its history of one hundred and forty years. Yet such has come to be a fact. In this battle for liberty, as we have had to mobilize our fighting manhood, our industrial power, our food power, so we have had to mobilize our money power to a degree hitherto undreamed of. Here we find the fifth element of the problem that confronted our country when we accepted Germany's challenge—how to pay the enormous cost of the struggle. Not so long since we thought we talked largely when we spoke of millions in relation to national finance. To-day we speak undismayed in terms of billions. We are told that in the year 1918–19 we shall spend as a nation more then $24,000,000,000, and we accept the situation with complacence.

Before the present conflict began it was a common theory that another great war in the world was unlikely, because it could be prevented by the bankers. It was known that hostilities under modern conditions would be enormously costly, and it was calculated that no nation, however rich, would be able to bear the financial burden of their long continuance. Germany had the correct idea of war finance. She prepared herself for war as no other nation had ever prepared, and attacked her neighbors suddenly. Her expenses were to be paid by her victims, through the robbery of their territories and indemnities. Germany, as usual, misread human nature. She found the victims of her aggression ready to go down into their pockets for their last cent, and into their larders for their last bone, to thwart her foul purposes. A beaten Germany may see a nation whose national income will be hard put to it to pay the interest on her national debt. Fortunately for her, this debt is owed almost entirely at home. Unquestionably there have been times in late years when smouldering sparks of war have been prevented from bursting into full flame by action of the great financial centres, but when Germany thought she had her neighbors by the throat, no question of money could hold her back. As they have survived the struggle of the battle-field, so have they survived the struggle of the pocket-book, but their financial problem was growing more difficult, and had not America taken up arms with them, they might have been in sore straits, for with their own productive power declining, they were being compelled more and more to go abroad for food and munitions. They would soon have been hard-pressed for money with which to pay, as the trade balances were steadily against them. Our government, however, realized that for more than two years they had been valiantly fighting our battle as well as their own, and when we declared war on Germany, one of our first acts was to go to the aid of our allies financially, to place large credits at their disposal, and to protect them from the additional burden of mounting prices for the materials they needed. The Treasury Department reported on August 23, 1918, that since April 6, 1917, we had advanced to the Allies $6,089,064,750. This sum represented the money actually paid out. Under agreements with them the total credits established for their benefit amounted to $6,692,040,000, as follows: Great Britain, $3,345,000,000; France, $2,065,-000,000; Italy, $760,000,000; Russia, $325,000,-000; Belgium, $154,250,000; Greece, $15,790,-000; Cuba, $15,000,000; Serbia, $12,000,000. In one year we advanced to our friends more than five times the sum spent in an average year for the expenses of our government. This money has not, however, gone out of the country in the form of gold, the international medium of exchange. It is represented by great shipments of food and munitions, purchased through our government for the Allies, for which they have engaged themselves to pay when the war is over. We have been advancing them nearly $10,000,000 a day. Before our entrance into the war the great financial burden was borne by Great Britain, which was lending large sums to those engaged with her in fighting the Hun. This burden has fallen on our shoulders to a large extent. The figures involved in these loans would have staggered our imaginations a

few years ago, and we should have doubted our
ability to make them. But America has found
the money. It has found it in a far greater
sum. Americans have been pouring out their
treasure as well as their blood to assure the de-
feat of the arch-enemy of civilization.

A fine part of the German plot against the
world was to attack America when Europe lay
prostrate at Germany's feet. There is evidence
of this in the writings and speeches of hundreds
of her publicists, statesmen, and soldiers. Had
we not entered the war, it would not have taken
long for a victorious Germany to have found
cause for a quarrel with us. In fact she had
long been planning it. With the friendly acqui-
escence of England we have upheld the Monroe Doctrine for nearly a century. Germany
regards the Monroe Doctrine as an impudence,
and would have attacked it on the first opportunity. She would have sought to thrust her
horrid kultur down our throats, and then to
make us pay for it handsomely in indemnities.
Had we presevered in our long-standing policy of
non-interference in European affairs we should
probably have had, not so far in the future,

a fine war of our own on our hands, with the predatory German demanding indemnities. But Americans found that the frontiers of their liberty lay on the battle-fields of Europe, and upset the German scheme. Since we went to war it has been common to hear the German press and German statesmen boastfully proclaiming their purpose to make us pay heavily for taking up arms against their country. To-day we pay billions for defense; we will not pay one cent for tribute.

The income of the American people in 1917 was slightly less than $50,000,000,000. In the last fiscal year before we declared war, ending June 30, 1916, the total receipts of the government were $1,153,044,639; the total disbursements were $1,072,894,093. In the year following, ending June 30, 1917, we had three months of war, and we find the total receipts, including the sale of Liberty Bonds, certificates of indebtedness, treasury notes, etc., $3,882,-068,710; the total expenditures, $3,083,476,791. Those three months of war increased the cost of our army from $164,635,576 to $440,276,880, and of our navy from $155,029,425 to $257,166,-

437. When one deals with such figures you abandon the cents, even though the Secretary of the Treasury records them.

The Sixty-Fourth Congress was generous to the navy and niggardly to the army. This Congress had in it many patriotic and far-seeing men, but they were hampered in their actions by dull-witted pacifists and pro-Germans. The Sixty-fifth Congress, which succeeded it almost immediately in special session, had in its membership some of the same dull-witted pacifists, and the pro-Germans turned Americans. We wonder if even the lady from Montana would to-day vote against war with the inventors of gas and liquid fire as a means of forwarding the aims of kultur. In the Sixty-fifth Congress, from the start, the patriotic and the far-seeing had their way. They were in a heavy majority. The dull-witted pacifists and the pro-Germans-turned-Americans did delay legislation on the selective-service law, but not for long. When it came to appropriations the administration had only to ask and it received. The loans to our allies were authorized. Issues of bonds, surpassing any sum we had ever dreamed of, were authorized. And rightly! It was no time to cavil over expenses. We had seen Belgium overrun and left ruined and starving; we had seen Serbia overrun and her population almost wiped out; Russia dissolving through Teuton intrigue into a state of anarchy; our old friend France standing with her back to the wall against the onrush of kultur's savages; and Britain, the Mother of Democracy, giving her children by the millions that the horrid Thing that had attacked the world might be killed. The Sixty-Fifth Congress has given the administration everything it asked for the prosecution of the war. The same house that argued so long over the selective-service law a little over a year later extended its provisions to include all men from 18 to 45, by a vote of 336 to 2. We have to-day, according to the German press, a crazy President, a crazy Congress, and a crazy people.

After we declared war, the government proceeded at once to the tremendous expansion of our army, navy, and merchant marine. No matter what the cost, the work had to be done. In framing its estimates of expenditures for the first year the government placed the figure at about $21,000,000,000, or nearly twice the sum that Great Britain had expended in any one year of the war. It happened, however, that the productive capacity of the country for war was not fully organized, and that while enormous orders of all kinds were placed, these orders could not be filled as rapidly as was expected. As a result, our expenditure in the first year of the war was some $8,000,000,000 less than the estimated figure. At the end of the fiscal year, June 30, 1918, the treasury reported that, including the money spent in the first three months of the war, it had disbursed, $13,915,-205,290. Of this sum nearly $5,623,029,750 was loaned to our allies.

The beginning of the present fiscal year found our war programme in full swing. Plans had been laid to double the size of our armies; warships and merchant ships were slipping from the ways and had to be paid for; ordnance in vast quantities was coming from our factories; our allies were calling for still more financial aid. The government presented to Congress its estimates of expenditures to June 30, 1919, and

Congress authorized the disbursement of the
enormous sum of more than $24,000,000,000.

How these appropriations have been apportioned is shown in the following table:

War Department..................	$14,073,671,181.88
Navy Department.................	1,616,550,360.77
Shipping Board...................	1,807,543,500.00
National defense.................	50,000,000.00
Federal control of transportation systems.....................	500,000,000.00
War Finance Corporation.........	500,000,000.00
Housing for war needs............	100,000,000.00
Loans to Allies...................	3,000,000,000.00
Interest on public debt............	588,049,168.00
Postal service....................	385,511,072.23
Deficiencies for prior years........	727,567,797.35
For all other purposes............	989,455,184.31
	$24,338,348,264.54

The total represents one-half of the income of
the American people. It means that one-half
the productive energy of the people will go to
the prosecution of the war. It has been pointed
out by certain experts in finance that it may be
found impossible to spend so great a sum, as
what we can spend is limited by what we can
produce, and we are already feeling a scarcity
of both material and labor. It has been con-

tended that it will be easier for the American
people to raise these vast sums than to spend
them; that the great problem will not be to
find the money, but to produce the war material
for which it pays.

It has long been an axiom of government that
wars must be paid for largely out of the people's
future earnings; that the generation that fights
a war must in part be relieved of the financial
burden by the generations that will profit by
the victory. To raise a war's entire cost by
taxation would disrupt a country's business.
It has been considered sound policy to raise the
money needed by loans; to raise by increased
taxation the money to pay the interest on the
loans, and to constitute a fund with which to
pay them off when they fall due. Of the $13,-
000,000,000 spent by our government in the
past year of the war, more than two-thirds was
raised by the sale of Liberty Bonds. About
$4,000,000,000 was secured by income and ex-
cess profits taxes and the usual forms of revenue. When for the second year of the war
Congress authorized the expenditure of almost
double the sum spent in the first year, it was

deemed advisable to double the income received
by the government from taxation, and this was
done by greatly increasing the imposts on the
incomes of business enterprises and private persons, and imposing special forms of taxation.
With $8,000,000,000 secured from taxation, there
remained to be obtained from the sale of bonds
about $16,000,000,000 in the present fiscal year.
This was a task to tax any people, however
rich they might be, but the record of Americans in the previous Liberty Loan campaigns
left no doubt that they would meet the issue.

We are raising a larger proportion of our war
expenses by taxation than are our allies, and
we are spending much more money. The total
cost of the war to Great Britain from August,
1914, to January 1, 1918, was $20,465,000,000,
besides which she had lent to her allies some
$6,500,000,000. Of this she has raised 18.33
per cent by taxation. In the same period
France spent $20,637,800,000, of which she
raised 15.8 per cent by taxation. Italy, in the
war up to January 1, 1918, spent $6,077,378,000,
of which she raised 11.8 per cent by taxation.
Germany had spent, in the same time, $24,129,-
000,000, of which she raised less than 4 per cent

Selling Liberty Bonds in front of the Sub-Treasury, New York City.

"Of the $13,000,000,000 spent by our government in the past year of the war, more than two-thirds was raised by the sale of Liberty Bonds."

by added taxes on her people. As to whether or not it is good policy for us to raise so large a proportion of our war costs by taxation is a question on which there are wide differences of opinion. American business men and the American people have more than met the government half-way in their willingness, both to pay and to lend. It is vital to the success of our army and navy that enterprise be encouraged and that we produce to the limit of our capacity. But too heavy imposts on business tend to a discouragement of enterprise and a curtailment of production. The policy of our government has been to pay the cost of the war out of our present income, as far as is possible, without disrupting business. To secure such a result requires exceedingly delicate adjustment.

Even the securing of one-third of the money needed by taxation still leaves a vast sum to be raised by loans, sixteen times what was required for our government in normal years. But the appeal to the people to show their patriotism by lending their money has in every instance met with a hearty response. The loans have all been oversubscribed. Before the first Liberty Loan was put out there were in the country only 400,000 holders of bonds. Our government securities were practically all held by the banks. The vast number of our people did not know what a bond was, and the loan campaigns proved themselves of value in the inculcation of lessons of thrift and of finance as well as of patriotism. To the first issue there were 4,500,000 subscribers; to the second, double that number; to the third 17,000,000 Americans subscribed. This means that one person in every six of our population is the holder of a government obligation. An analysis of the figures shows a progressive increase in the number of small subscriptions. Of the first loan 23 per cent was represented by purchases of less than $10,000; of the second, 29 per cent; of the third 47 per cent.

The record of the people, in response to the call of the government to lend it their money, is shown in this table:

	SUBSCRIBED	ALLOTTED
First Liberty Loan	$3,035,226,850	$2,000,000,000
Second Liberty Loan.....	4,617,532,300	3,808,766,150
Third Liberty Loan......	4,170,019,650	4,170,019,650

The fact that of the second loan, more than 12,000,000 bonds of the denomination of $100 and $50 were purchased gives evidence of the degree to which persons with small incomes participated.

With their men fighting so gallantly on the fields of France and on the sea, Americans will not stint to support them with their treasure. They will ask, though, for the sake of those very men, that the money be carefully and wisely spent. In the main it has been. In the expenditure of sums so vast there are likely to be cases of recklessness and extravagance. According to the Senate Investigating Committee millions were wasted on the aircraft programme, many millions spent and few fighting planes placed on the front. Before another year the millions put into aircraft production will tell, though it was unfortunate that, through lack of foresight, they must tell so late. But it is well to remember that, while the War Department failed to do well with the money placed in its hands for aerial warfare, with the money given to it to raise, equip and transport armies to the battle-front it has done much. It has seen to it that, as a whole, our fighting men are well clothed, well fed, and well quartered.

Our soldiers and sailors are paid as are the men of no other country, and the government has arranged that proper provision is made for them or their dependants in event of death or disability. It is now conducting in the Treasury Department the greatest insurance company in the world. The department's Bureau of War Risk Insurance, as now carried on, is the outgrowth of the need of protecting our merchant marine at the outbreak of the European War. The government had then to take cognizance of the fact that the risks of war made it impossible for our ship owners to secure proper insurance at anything but prohibitive rates. By act of Congress, approved September 2, 1914, the government undertook to insure these vessels at reasonable rates. Then the dangers of the sea made it difficult for the vessels to get crews, and by an act of June 12, 1917, the operations of the bureau were extended to insure the crews of these ships. The price of insurance for a man in our army or navy was prohibitive in a private company. It was found that these companies would charge $580 a year for a $10,000 policy on the life of a soldier or sailor, and a private serving in France receives only $396 a year. Under a law passed on October 6, 1917, the government will insure any soldier or sailor against death or total disability up to the sum of $10,000, in multiples of $500 at the same rate, practically, that they would pay to an insurance company in peace times. The charge for this insurance is deducted from his monthly pay. The treasury bears the cost of administration and the excess mortality and disability cost resulting from the hazards of war. A statement of the Treasury Department shows that on August 1, 1918, nearly 3,000,000 applications for insurance had been received, representing a total of more than $25,000,000,000, in average policies of $8,511.

Such a provision is certainly just to the men who are fighting the country's battles. Further, to insure their ease of mind regarding their dependent families, the government makes what are known as family allotments. The enlisted man must allot $15 monthly to his wife and children, which is withheld from his pay by the

government. To this the government adds
$15 monthly to the wife; where there is a wife
and one child, $25; a wife and two children,
$32.50, and $5 for each additional child. Provision is made in this way for motherless
children and for dependent parents. Under
another section of the law the government pro-
tects itself against the evils that grew up under the old pension system, and at the same
time makes clear to the fighting man just what
his dependants will receive in case of his death,
or what he will receive in event of disability
incurred in the service. Every contingency is
carefully provided for. The sums granted are
not large. A widow, for example, will receive
$25 monthly; if she has a child, $35; if two
children, $47.50, with $5 for each additional
child. But it is considered that such sums,
with the insurance added, should provide comfortably for the soldiers' families.

Besides its task of collecting and disbursing
vast sums of money, and of conducting an insurance business on a scale hitherto unheard of,
the work of the Treasury Department has been
greatly increased by new duties thrown on it

by various acts of Congress. Even before we went to war, the Federal Farm Loan law was in operation, with Federal Land Banks established in twelve districts of the country. These banks, through their agencies, have been lending money on farm mortgages and have proved valuable in stimulating food production since we went to war. In 1917 more than $20,000,000 was loaned by these banks for the furtherance of agricultural projects, and in the present year this sum will be exceeded. The War Finance Board, of which the Secretary of the Treasury is chairman, was created by an act of April 5, 1918. It has a capital stock of a $500,000,-000, all owned by the government, and its function is to aid by advances of money those businesses whose operation is necessary to the conduct of the war. The same act also established the "Capital Issues Committee," which acts to curb the expansion of unnecessary enterprises, by supervising the issue of new securities of amounts greater than $100,000. The government has held that unnecessary enterprises must be curbed, and that it will need for its own uses every dollar that can be saved. It is easy to understand this view. Our expenditures are now running at the rate of $2,000,000,000 monthly. If the war lasts until the end of 1919, we shall have to spend $50,-000,000,000. To raise so great a sum all the energies of the American people will be needed.

CHAPTER XII

LABOR

OBVIOUSLY we cannot keep our ships afloat and our vast armies overseas unless the industries of the country are organized on a war basis and operated by an army of patriotic men. It is estimated that it requires all the labor of at least three men to keep one fighting man at the front. This figure is small. But accepting it, we see that to keep an army of 5,000,000 men fighting we must have 15,000,000 at home working solely for the soldiers. As a matter of fact, we are expending half of our national income on war work, and, therefore, half of our working energy. The problem of organizing the country's labor-power that it might be used to the best advantage becomes one of the most difficult of the intricate problems faced by the government.

Before we entered the war the urgent needs of the fighting nations brought them to our markets for food and materials of all kinds,

and the result of their competitive bidding for
these things was a rapid rise in prices at home
and a startling increase in the costs of living.
Large profits were to be made in these foreign
contracts and the manufacturers and producers began bidding against one another for
labor, a process which resulted in greatly increased wage scales. Factories not engaged
in highly profitable war work, and the farms,
found great difficulty in securing workers, and
to be able to pay the advanced rates had to
increase the prices of their products. And so
the withdrawal of millions of men and women
from productive occupations in Europe brought
to us a parallel rising of wages and prices.
Some employers made great profits and there
was a resulting spirit of unrest among employees, who felt that they were not getting
their full share of the results of their labor.
This feeling found expression in frequent strikes.
Industries which had no share in these great
profits felt this unrest severely. Of this situation the railroads afford the best example. In
1916 their employees demanded the establishment of an eight-hour day and time and a half

pay for overtime. To avoid a nation-wide strike, in September Congress passed the Adamson law, compelling the roads to make an eight-hour day the standard of pay and to pay pro rata for overtime. This greatly increased their expenses although their earnings were at the time steadily declining. The government did grant them some relief by allowing an increase in freight rates. This dispute between the companies and their men threatened trouble enough for the country in times of peace. It continued up almost to the very moment of our entry into the war. Similar controversies were recurring from time to time in other industries.

When we entered the war we had to produce ships, munitions, and food in unprecedented quantities, and the continuation of controversies between employers and employees was a grave threat to the success of our fighting men. The control of the large employers was a comparatively easy matter. The great majority of them placed their plants at the disposal of the government and entered into voluntary agreements as to the prices they should receive for

their products.   Any profiteering was prevented
by tax laws which took from them the largest
part of their earnings above what they had
made in normal times.   The control of the great
army of labor, organized and unorganized, a
great deal of it floating, was another matter.
But steps had to be taken to prevent, as far as
possible, any halting in production.

When the war-cloud was hanging over us,
after the break in diplomatic relations with Germany, the Advisory Commission of the Council of National Defense was formed, and Samuel
Gompers, president of the American Federation
of Labor, took a place upon it as labor's representative.   On March 12 a meeting of the
representatives of all the unions was held in
Washington, and these leaders pledged their
loyalty to the country in event of war and
called on their fellow workers to follow their
example.   The day after war was declared Mr.
Gompers pledged the support of the federation
to the government, and the federation, in its
annual convention on November 12, affirmed
its belief in the war as essential to the defense
of democracy.   So the representatives of the

greatest body of organized laborers have from the first proved themselves loyal and behind the government in the prosecution of the war, in recognition of which the administration has placed a number of them in places of responsibility. Mr. Gompers formed a labor committee of some 350 persons to act with the Council of National Defense. This committee included representatives of the government, capital, and labor, and it was divided into eight subcommittees, having charge of the various phases of the problem. The main work, however, was done through an executive committee of fourteen, acting as advisory to the council.

The American Federation, which thus came so promptly to the support of the war, is the largest organized labor body in the country, comprising some 111 national unions, organized in the crafts and industries. It has a membership of nearly 2,500,000. Other so-called labor bodies, however, did not prove themselves so patriotic. One of these, the Industrial Workers of the World, with headquarters in Chicago, carried on a campaign to hamper industry and block the selective-service law. Its operations were largely in the lumber regions and on the farms of the West, where there is a large migratory working population. So disloyal were its activities that the government had finally to arrest more than 200 of its leaders in various parts of the country, and in August of this year the largest number of these were convicted in the courts and sentenced to long terms in prison.

The Socialist party of America is a political organization whose membership comes largely from the ranks of labor. Immediately after the declaration of war, it held a convention in St. Louis, went on record against the action of the government, and called on "all workers to refuse to support their governments in their wars." It further demanded unyielding opposition to the proposed draft law. The action was not unanimous. A considerable number of members withdrew from the party, and at a meeting later in Chicago formed the National party, which, while its platform was socialistic, declared its loyalty to the government in the prosecution of the war. But the Socialist party carried on a continuous campaign, hampering the government in many ways, compelling the authorities to take vigorous action to suppress its activities.

We have seen the leaders of the greatest of the labor organizations giving the government their support from the beginning of the war. They have given it loyally. They have frowned down the German-made efforts to have conferences at The Hague and Stockholm of international representatives of the world's workers for the purpose of agitating a peace which would be to the advantage of Germany. They have declared steadily for the prosecution of the war to a finish, to the end of German autocracy and militarism. Their position has not been an easy one. However good their intentions, they have often had trouble with their locals, which have used the necessities of the government in the war as a club with which to enforce their demands.

On the advice of Mr. Gompers the Council of National Defense, on April 7, 1917, adopted a report urging that no changes in existing standards of labor be made either by employers or employees during the war, without its approval. A few days later this was modified by an exception that no changes of wages should be sought by either party through strikes or lockouts without giving the government an opportunity to settle the difficulties without a stoppage of work. It was hoped that employers and employees would live up to these arrangements, but the figures available show that the first year of the war was marked by a great number of strikes. The report of the Department of Labor shows that between April 6 and October 19, 1917, 211 strikes had been called to its attention. An unofficial record of strikes between April 6 and December 15 shows that 529 occurred, involving 126,400 employees to the loss of 3,234,446 man days of work. In the shipyards alone, prior to December 26 there were strikes involving 596,992 lost man days. In the first year of the war there were referred to the Department of Labor for adjudication 936 labor disputes, of which 440 had reached the strike stage. The conciliators settled all of these but 73. But it is evident that the government's no-strike programme was a failure.

The situation in the labor world in the first year of the war was chaotic, and between strikes and a lack of co-ordination of the various government departments, war work was greatly hampered. There was no orderly system of apportioning the available labor. The army had taken millions of men and labor was scarce. One shipyard with urgent contracts would bid higher wages and take the men employed in another near by. Munition works would draw men from the shipyards, and shipyards from the munition works. Government departments were bidding against each other for men. Skilled men were shifting about the country in search of the highest pay, and much valuable time was lost in this turnover. Where disputes occurred with the men they were settled by the individual department or munition plant, without regard to the general needs of the government.

It was evident that the government had to take cognizance of these conditions, and late in April, 1918, the National War Labor Board was constituted. Two of its members, William H. Taft and Frank P. Walsh, represent the

public; the other ten represent equally employers and employees. Its functions are "to
bring about a settlement by mediation and
conciliation of every controversy between employers and employees in the field of production necessary for the effective conduct of the
war." This board since its formation has been
kept busy settling disputes. It has no real
power to enforce decisions against labor, other
than that of patriotic appeal. In many cases
this has proved effective. There is always a tendency where disputes over wages are involved
to grant a higher scale, and where shop regulations are concerned to favor the demands of
the union. It is the easiest way to avoid difficulty, however hard it may be on the employer. Employees who are dissatisfied with the
decisions can strike and sometimes they have
done so. Five thousand machinists at Bridge-
port recently went out because they objected
to the board's award of an increase in wages
to all employees receiving under seventy-eight
cents an hour, but establishing no increase
above that rate. This strike ended only when
the President made a personal appeal to the

From a photograph by Underwood and Underwood.

Patriotic rally for ship-builders in hull of a wooden ship building at Seattle, Washington.
The speaker, a representative of the U. S. Department of Labor, is urging the men to stand by the government.

loyalty of the men and warned them that those who persisted in striking would not be employed in any other government work. This strike delayed for two weeks work on thousands of machine-guns so urgently needed by the soldiers who are fighting our battles. Dissatisfied employers can do little. They cannot strike and the government has power to take over their plants. Recently a large munition company asked the government to take over its factories, maintaining that it could not manage its business efficiently on the lines laid down by the board for the dealings with the employees.

As regards labor, the country is on the horns of a dilemma. Every rise in the cost of living is followed by a demand for—in fact, a need of—higher wages. Every time wages rise the cost of living goes up.

The railroads are a case in point. In the years 1916 and 1917 the railroads increased wages of their employees approximately $350,-000,000 a year. In the same period their earnings were strictly limited by the rate rulings of the Interstate Commerce Commission, and they were hard put to it to find money for needed improvements in lines and rolling-stock. After we went to war, with the co-operation of the government, their operation was unified under the charge of a committee of executives known as the Railroads War Board. This board did much to increase the efficiency of the roads, but the demands of the war greatly increased the traffic and there was at times great congestion. In November the trainmen and conductors began to agitate for an increase of forty per cent in pay, and a situation similar to that at the time of the passage of the Adamson law might have been created, had not the government stepped in, and acting under the authority of Congress, taken control of the roads. This was done to insure still more efficient operation, and to secure this the government had to make large advances in money for the improvement of the lines. The President by proclamation took over the railroads on December 26, and placed their operation in the hands of William G. McAdoo, Secretary of the Treasury, as director-general. The government was at once met with the persistent wage problem, and after an investigation of living costs granted advances of wages to all employees receiving less than $250 per month. This added $300,000,000 a year to the cost of operating the roads. The increase in other expenses aggregated more than $500,000,000 more. To meet these heavy new charges the director-general had to order a 25-per-cent increase in all freight rates and an advance in passenger rates from 2½ to 3 cents per mile. Such increases added to the general cost of living.

The government had to act to hold down the cost of living, to stabilize wages, and to control labor as far as possible that it might be used to its greatest productive capacity. The first it did through its system of price-fixing. For the better control of labor it organized the War Labor Policies Board in the Department of Labor, which has the direction and distribution of the labor-supply during the war. An important part of this administration's work is done through the United States Employment Service. This bureau has established branches throughout the country and has formed the United States Public Service Reserve in which are enlisted many thousands of workmen. When the army, navy, or Shipping Board need workmen they apply to the Employment Service, and the men are supplied from the districts nearest the plants where they are wanted, thus avoiding the unnecessary movement of men for long distances. The employment bureau has lists of nearly every available man in the country for war work, and is kept advised of the needs of the yards and factories. It sees to it that the vital industries get the men they need and its operations have ended the old expensive system of competitive bidding for labor. It has organized so as to have its representatives in every county of the country hunting up available men. It has encroached heavily on the unessential industries, but even the managers of these have largely given it patriotic help, as it is generally realized that the conduct of the war industries is vital to the nation's safety. The War Labor Policies Board decides directly for war industries and indirectly for non-war industries questions involving distribution of labor, wages, hours, and working conditions. Non-war industries can be prevented from using labor unnecessarily through the pressure of the War Industries Board and the Fuel Administration which control the supplies of raw materials and coal. The government has established a grip on industry that would not have been thought possible a few years ago.

One of the necessities of the situation is that wages be stabilized as far as possible. Higher wages in one part of the country than another means constant migration and a consequent loss in production. To this end the Labor Policies Board has been bending its energy. It has to consider the living costs and conditions in any particular locality and to fix standards of pay that will as far as possible discourage migration. It must strive, too, to create such conditions of labor as will make for contentment and prevent unrest. The function of the War Labor Board is to mediate in disputes between employer and employees, when they occur. The function of the Labor Policies Board is to try to prevent the occurrence of such controversies.

By the end of the present year we shall have withdrawn from our industries more than 5,000,000 of our best men to serve in our army and navy. Immigration has stopped and our farms and factories are being called on to produce as never before. The work must be done if our men at the front and our allies who are fighting with them have what they need to crush the German menace forever. To do it we have only the man-power left within our own borders. As the government has called on Americans to save food for our soldiers and our allies and to save money for our treasury, so it has called on them to work. Soon there will be few families in this country who have not some one dear to them fighting on the fields of France. Americans will as little brook the slackers in work as they have those who have been slackers in the fight.

The vast majority of the laborers of the country have showed themselves loyal to the core. This means the vast majority of Americans, for nearly every American is a worker, no matter what his social status. From railroads, farms, and shops, the stores and offices, the men have gone willingly to fight in defense of our freedom. But organized labor is a class of labor by itself. It comprises but a comparatively small part of the community, and yet it has always been the special pet of politicians of all parties. They, in their appeals for votes, usually speak of the class as though no one else ever worked. They draw a line between employer and employee, which would indicate that the employer was free from all care and labor. When we went to war there was much talk of profiteering by the makers of munitions. Yet the treasury figures show that at that time only one-half of the munition-makers had made enough profits to bring them in the reach of the drastic excess profits tax. The legislation that was passed to speed up our war industries was aimed to give the government power solely over the employers and plants. Nothing was done to insure a steady effort by labor, other than as it would be obtained by raising wages and appeals to patriotism. The principle has been, if a demand for higher pay is made, to tell the employer he must pay more without telling him where is he to get the money. In the case of the railroads it was easy, because here the government had simply to take control and tax the public to find the needed funds. When a dispute arose between the telegraph companies and their employees, and the companies' officers felt the decision of the War Labor Board to be unfair, the government again took control. And again it can raise wages and tax the public. The position of a munition-maker, who is working for the government on a cost, plus a commission, basis is safe. He can meet all advances in wages ordered by the government mediators, and the government will pay the added cost. But the employer who has a contract to deliver at a fixed price may at times find himself in a way of losing money if he agrees to an award of higher wages. Yet, if he refuses, he is likely to have the government take over his plant, and worse, to find himself called unpatriotic.

The national leaders of organized labor have patriotically done their best to prevent strikes and the consequent interruption of vital production. The principle of mediation by government agencies was adopted, as we have seen; but the War Labor Board has little power to enforce its decrees, except that the government can act directly against one party to the dispute in question and only indirectly against the other. The authority of the national labor leaders cannot be extended to the non-union labor, which is the largest element, and their influence over organized labor has sometimes proved not great. It is unfortunate that certain classes of organized and unorganized labor should have seized upon the country's hour of necessity to profiteer. Where the conditions of labor are wrong, they should be righted, and the government has made every effort to see that this is done. But the day when every ship that leaves the ways means a nearer ending of the war, and every gun that goes over the sea gives protection to our gallant fighting men, is no time for strikes in industries essential to the prosecution of the war, or to allow such strikes.

CHAPTER XIII

THE COUNCIL OF NATIONAL DEFENSE

ONE of the most important elements in our mobilization has been the work of the Council of National Defense. It is this great body of volunteer workers that helped to bring order out of chaos in the early days of the war. Strictly speaking, the council is a committee of six, the Secretaries of War, Navy, Interior, Agriculture, Commerce, and Labor. Actually it is more than that. It is a large body of men and women, every one possessing special knowledge in some branch of industry or war work which they have placed at the service of the government. When our relations with Germany were growing strained in 1916, Congress passed an act forming the council. This act, approved August 29, provided that the cabinet members named should form a body to act for "the co-ordination of industries and resources for national security and welfare." It provided that the council should name an advisory committee of not more than seven persons, each of whom had some special knowledge that would be of service to the country in event of war. These persons were to serve without compensation. The advisory committee was not organized until the following March, when the war-cloud was growing heavier. As formed, its members were: Daniel Willard, transportation and communication, chairman; Howard E. Coffin, aircraft; Julius Rosenwald, supplies (including clothing), etc.; Bernard M. Baruch, raw materials, minerals, and metals; Doctor Hollis Godfrey, engineering and education; Samuel Gompers, labor, including conservation of health and welfare of workers; Doctor Franklin Martin, medicine and surgery, including general sanitation.

Walter S. Gifford was made director and Grosvenor B. Clarkson, secretary of the council and advisory commission, and they act as connecting-link between the two.

The principal duties of the council are:

To supervise and direct investigation, and

make recommendations to the President and the heads of executive departments as to:

The location of railroads with reference to the frontier of the United States, so as to render possible expeditious concentration of troops and supplies.

The mobilization of military and naval resources for defense.

The increase of domestic production of articles and materials essential to the support of armies and of the people during the interruption of foreign commerce.

The development of seagoing transportation.

Amounts, location, method, and means of production and availability of military supplies.

The giving of information to producers and manufacturers as to the class of supplies needed by the government, and the creation of relations which will render possible the immediate concentration and utilization of the resources of the nation.

Reports to the President or to the heads of executive departments upon special inquiries or subjects appropriate thereto.

The outbreak of war brought to Washington a great number of men and women, having special knowledge in the various phases of industry and science, who volunteered to serve the government without compensation. With them, under the direction of the council, was formed a great organization of several thousand volunteers, which has been of the highest service to the country. The leading railroad men, manufacturers, scientists, and labor leaders have been serving patriotically, and their advice has been of incalculable value. There were formed committees on munitions, raw materials, finished products, coal production, women's defense work, labor, scientific research, surgery, and numerous other subjects, with under them subcommittees working with details. To give advice has been practically their main function, but they have also generated many new ideas which have been put into operation with effect. The advisory commission and its subordinate committees have no mandatory powers. They merely study the problems presented to them and make their recommendations to the council which acts upon them. When any problem requiring special knowledge arises, it is submitted to the Advisory Commission which gives it to the special branch of the organization competent to study the matter and make recommendations. The construction of the cantonments is an example. When the War Department was confronted with that great work, it called on the council for aid. A committee on emergency construction was formed, and a number of engineers and builders served on it, working in conjunction with the department. On the committees, to secure closer co-ordination, representatives of the government departments concerned have had representatives. Thus, for the first year of the war an aircraft programme was in charge of the Aircraft Production Board, acting through the Signal Corps of the army and the Construction Bureau of the navy.

Under the council's supervision subsidiary bodies, Councils of National Defense, have been organized in every State in the Union. They collect information that is of service to the government and carry on campaigns of education and patriotism.

One of the most important accomplishments of the council was the organization of what is now our great War Industries Board, which has such wide powers affecting the mobilization of our resources for war purposes. At first the work now done by this board was in the hands of the raw material and finished material divisions and of the General Munitions Board. The operations of these bodies were found to be cumbersome, and in July, 1917, they were merged into the War Industries Board, with seven members, representing the army, the navy, industry, and labor. Its duties were to assign priorities among the government departments and the allied governments in their demands on our industries; to advise as to supplies of materials and labor; to advise as to prices; to secure the co-operation of industry and labor; to prevent the enhancement of prices and confusion of industry. While the change proved beneficial, neither the administration nor Congress was satisfied with the workings of the system. Congress proposed a ministry of munitions. To this the President objected, as he felt that the powers of the members would be too much limited. He asked for authority to create bodies which could act quickly and without red tape. At his request, the Overman Bill was passed, giving him authority to form boards to conduct the war work in accordance with the needs of the moment. He appointed Bernard M. Baruch chairman of the War Industries Board with large powers, and that board became at once almost a separate department of the government. Mr. Baruch had been head of the raw material division of the Defense Council and had had great success in the early part of the war on securing much-needed supplies of copper, steel, zinc, lead, platinum, and other metals at prices far below the market levels. In his capacity as adviser to the government in the purchase of these supplies, he was met half-way by the producers. The heads of all the great producing companies placed their plants at the government's service and agreed to furnish their products to the government at prices far less than they were commanding in the open market. Nitrates for the making of explosives, manganese and tungsten for our steel mills, many other metals and chemicals needed for our war industries he, with foresight, secured at reasonable cost.

What the President established in the War Industries Board, with Mr. Baruch at its head, was practically a clearing-house for all government and Allied purchases. The chairman has associated with him eight men, all experts in their particular duties, and under the board has been built up a great business organization, with every branch in charge of a specialist. The board keeps close watch on all industries in the country, and knows where all supplies are to be found and how great they are. The departments no longer bid against each other. They still make their own contracts but not until they have consulted the board and had the supplies allotted to them in accordance with the priority of their needs. Working with the Railroad Administration, the board decides what commodities shall be moved over the lines, for so great is the congestion of traffic that it is essential that priority be given to special supplies. It has to keep in touch with the War Trade Board, since the scarcity of shipping necessitates careful supervision over our imports of raw materials. It has to work, too, in close co-operation with the Fuel Administration to see that industries vital to our war programme receive coal.

The requirements division of the board meets daily. These sessions are attended by the heads of all the chief sections and representatives of the various government departments and of the Allied Purchasing Commission. Statements are laid before it outlining the needs of every branch of the government and of our allies in the way of raw and finished materials. The available supply of every commodity concerned can be quickly ascertained from the section in charge of it. The government, if necessary, takes the entire supply and the board allots it. In this manner co-ordination and rapid action have been obtained.

The board has no specific power in law to fix prices. The prices to be paid by the government are agreed on between the Price Fixing Committee of the board and representatives of the producers. The government only intervenes to fix prices to the public where it has taken so large a part of any commodity as to create a scarcity for the civil population. Here the price is also fixed by agreement with the producer and it must be the same for the government, the Allies, and the civilian. The commodity is apportioned among them according to their needs. The wholesaler or retailer who gets a share must sell it at the government's figure. If he does not he goes on the black list and receives nothing of the later distributions. But in general there has been wide-spread co-operation with the government by producers and dealers. The government has the power to commandeer and operate the industries essential to the war, but with hands full operating its army and navy, it has chosen the wiser method of trusting to the patriotism of the business men and securing the benefit of their energy and intelligence. They have responded to this call in full measure.

As our industries have sent their representatives to Washington to help the government, so have our sciences. Immediately on the outbreak of war, the National Research Council affiliated itself with the Council of National

Defense, as its agency in science and research. This council is organized in a series of divisions, which draw together into small groups the representatives of the various special committees dealing with different branches of the mathematical, physical and biological sciences, engineering, medicine, agriculture, and various arts. For example, its engineering division was organized with the co-operation of the national engineering societies, who are represented on the executive board. Under this division are sections on metallurgy, mechanical, electrical, and other branches of engineering. In order to avoid unnecessary duplication, the National Advisory Committee for aeronautics acts as a section on aeronautics in this division.

The council has headquarters in Washington, which are in charge of Doctor George E. Hale, a well-known astronomer. In this office the work is centralized. Problems are brought to it by the various departments of the government, and they are at once assigned for study to the division of the council concerned. As nearly every scientist of note in the country is associated with the body, the government has quickly at its service the highest of ability. As in the case of the Naval Consulting Board, the council has made public but little of the results of its researches and inventions. A full report will not be made until after the war. It is permitted, however, to speak of a few of these which give an idea of the nature of its service.

The question of helmets and body armor was one which arose at the beginning of the war. At the request of the War Department a special committee was appointed to study this subject, with Doctor Bashford Dean, curator of armor in the Metropolitan Museum of New York, at its head. Associated with him were engineers and metallurgists. This committee worked out a new form of helmet, in which work the experience of Doctor Dean and his knowledge of old forms proved invaluable. Doctor Henry M. Howe studied the metallurgical side of the problem, selecting the best steel for the head-piece, and making tests with machine-guns on the steel in various forms, both in sheets and in the shape which it has been given in the helmet. The helmet thus devised is being made in large numbers and is in use in our army. From this problem the committee went on to the subject of body armor. This seems like harking back to mediæval days and outworn devices. But experience has shown that in modern fighting a large percentage of the wounds are made by low-velocity bullets and bits of shrapnel which have nearly spent themselves. To devise a steel protection for the breast and legs to resist these is not difficult, but the breastplate and leg guards must be so light as not to impede the movements of the soldier. The committee has devised such armor pieces as light as possible, and yet sufficiently resistant to low-velocity bullets and shell fragments to be effective. It is being tried on the fields of France by our men.

The problems that have been submitted to the council for solution have been almost innumerable. This war has been one of science, and every branch of science has been engaged in the combat. One of the most difficult of these problems has been to find means of locating submarines under water and destroying them. The headway attained here has not been made known, but it is known that there has been headway. Another complex problem was to devise an accurate method of dropping bombs from airplanes. In the early stages of the war, this was done in random fashion, and it was difficult to sight and hit a target. The question involves the trajectory of the bomb as it falls from a fast-flying plane. The council brought into co-operation with the Signal Corps and the Ordnance Department, both of which were engaged in this investigation, various mathematical physicists whose previous experience adapted them for this work. Some of the most interesting results were obtained by a mathematical astronomer of Princeton, who utilized, for calculating the trajectories of bombs, certain new methods which were developed for the purpose of calculating planetary orbits. This same astronomer derived the quickest known method of reducing the observations made for the location of guns by the method of sound ranging.

Doctor Hale has pointed out that there is

great similarity between some of the problems of aerial warfare and astronomy. An example which he gives is the photographing of trenches from an airplane. There is always more or less dust or haze in the air which interferes with photography. By using a color-screen in front of the camera, and thus by cutting off the violet and blue part of the light and letting through the red, yellow, green and light-blue parts of the spectrum, the operator is able to get increased contrast and make the trenches show better; the best photographs are made with the aid of color-screens. In astronomy, when you want to photograph the sun, if you photograph it directly, you get just what you see with your eye, but if you want to bring out the invisible phenomena of the sun's atmosphere, you use simply a refinement of that method. You photograph with a single line of the spectrum, say a line of hydrogen, and thus render visible the entire hydrogen atmosphere of the sun, otherwise wholly invisible. This is the same principle that the man in the airplane uses when he photographs the trenches.

Among the accomplishments of the Research

Council has been a new range-finder developed by a well-known physicist, and an ear-protector by the same scientist. The navy has adopted a new method of selecting and training gunners which was developed by a psychologist. It makes it possible to judge how accurately a man may be expected to point a gun and tests his ability as a marksman. The army has adopted a system of psychological tests to determine the mental ability of the individual soldier, which was evolved through the co-operation of the Research Council and the American Psychological Association. Another scientist has devised a method of testing on the ground the ability of an aviator to rise to very high altitudes, thus making it possible to judge accurately just how high a man can fly without being in danger of heart-failure and fainting-spells, in which he would plunge to his death.

The council has dealt with many questions in chemistry, both in research on problems of importance from a military or industrial point of view and in furnishing information on chemical subjects to the War Industries Board.   Perhaps the most important single problem in chemistry connected with the war is that of the fixation of nitrogen from the air. Nitrates are needed both for high explosives and for fertilizers, so the problem has both military and industrial aspects. Before the war all nitrates used in this country were imported from Chile, and that supply might be cut off by the activities of German agents or in other ways. Germany, foreseeing this long ago, developed methods for the fixation of nitrogen, and utilizing the cheap water-power of Norway for this purpose, established very extensive plants under German control. Subsequently, new methods for the fixation of nitrogen were worked out by the German chemists, and since the beginning of the war ample supplies of nitrates have been produced in Germany by these processes. In this country, at the request of the Secretary of War in May, 1916, the council appointed a committee to report on the best methods of nitrogen fixation with a view to the best utilization of an appropriation of twenty million dollars, which was made that summer by Congress for the erection of plants for this purpose. Since that time much larger appropriations for the same purpose have been made, and several of these plants are in operation. At present a committee of the council is assisting the Ordnance Department in the improvement of various processes which are easily open to important development through chemical experimentation. Here, as in all other cases, the fundamental principle of the council has been to recommend the immediate adoption of the best available process, and not to allow research development to retard in the slightest degree the immediate utilization of the best available methods to meet war necessities. At the same time research follows the application of these methods, especially in such a case as that of nitrogen fixation, where slight improvements might effect enormous savings in the process of manufacture.

As the business men and scientists of the country mobilized themselves for the service of the country, so did the medical men. The medical section of the Council of National Defense has done a notable work for the army and navy. Through its medium it has been possible for the government to keep in touch with the medical profession over the entire country, and to secure the thousands of men and women needed as surgeons and nurses. The section, too, has performed a valuable service in standardizing instruments and supplies, and in securing a substitution of instruments for those for which we formerly relied on Germany. The war has made a heavy drain on the medical and nursing professions, and to enlist their members in sufficient numbers in the national service, without unduly endangering the public health, has not been one of the least of the government's problems.

CHAPTER XIV

THE RAILROADS

IT has happened that in its battle against autocracy, our government has become an autocracy. But it has become an autocracy for the war only and by the wish of the people, as expressed through their representatives. This condition is true of every other nation that is fighting the German horror. Unified action was necessary, and unified action could only be had through a centralization of control. As the Allies placed their armies under the command of General Foch, so America placed her industries under command of President Wilson, that their co-ordinated powers might be used to the quick winning of the war. We have seen how our government has taken indirect control of our farms and their products through the activities of the Food Administration; how it controls our manufacturing industries through the War Industries Board and Fuel Administration. Although in all of these cases it has wide powers under the law, instead of using the force of the law to attain its ends it has relied more on suasion and on the patriotism of the people; it has endeavored to secure its desires by agreement instead of compulsion. The real power that it yields is in the fact that it is the largest buyer of commodities in the world. In every activity of our lives we see the hand of the government. Economic changes have been wrought by the war that a few years ago we should have deemed impossible. Of these many will pass away with the war. One change alone seems likely to continue, if not in all, in at least some of its phases. It is that in our transportation system. As the government had to take virtual control of our industries, so it had to take real control of our railroads. To do so was a necessity of war. Troops, food, material had to be moved in orderly fashion. Before the government took this control, the railroads could not attain the high pitch of efficiency that was needed, and the reasons were obvious.

We have the greatest transportation system in the world, and some ten years ago James

J. Hill, the veteran railroad builder, said that if our railroads were to be kept in condition and to keep pace with the country's growth, there would have to be expended on them one billion dollars a year. They were never allowed to make that billion. They were so regulated by the Interstate Commerce Commission that their earnings were kept to the lowest possible point, while taxes and the prices of labor and material were steadily rising. They were pinched between upper and nether millstones. To make extensions or improvements they had to borrow money. In 1914 and 1915 traffic on them fell to a point that brought trouble to many of them to meet expenses. They had no money with which to provide for future needs. In the fall of 1915, their business began to increase so rapidly that there was a serious shortage of rolling-stock. While their gross operating incomes increased largely, the net revenue per mile for the whole country decreased. In the fall of 1916, the employees began to agitate for an eight-hour day, with ten hours' pay, and time and one-half overtime. The refusal of the railroads to meet this, brought, as we have seen, the passage of the Adamson law giving the men an eight-hour day and pro rata overtime, and caused a controversy which continued almost to the day of our entering the war. The railroads appealed to the courts for relief. As late as March 17, the men were threatening to strike, and were only withheld by the efforts of the government and the national labor leaders who saw war ahead. When the decision of the Supreme Court two days later upheld the law, the dispute ended but only for a time. The Interstate Commerce Commission granted the railroads some relief in the way of increases in rates on certain commodities in various sections, but this proved inadequate. For several years there had been a continued depreciation in road-beds and rolling-stock, and no money to mend the trouble. Many of the roads had failed to pay the interest on money borrowed for improvements, and railroad credit was generally bad.

The war greatly increased the strain of our transportation systems. To secure co-ordination a Railroads War Board was formed, composed of six leading railroad executives, and they operated the roads for nine months as one, as far as they could with the restrictions placed on them by Federal and State laws. Despite the fact that in this time they handled a record-breaking traffic, the congestion became steadily worse, and in the fall of 1917 it threatened serious consequences. About this time the employees were again agitating for more wages. Some seventy thousand of them had gone into the army and navy, further handicapping the roads. Labor was scarce and it was hard to hold the men when high pay was to be had in the shipyards and munition factories. To end all these difficulties the President acted under the powers given him by Congress in the Adamson law, which allowed him to take over and operate the roads in case of military necessity. By proclamation, on December 26, 1917, he took control of the entire transportation system of the country, both by land and water.

The United States Railroad Administration was then formed, with Secretary McAdoo at its head. The administration is to operate the roads only for the period of the war and twenty-one months thereafter. Under the law passed on March 21, the roads must be maintained in as good repair and with as complete equipment as when taken over; the roads must receive in compensation a net income equal in every case to the average net income in the three years preceding June 30, 1917, which happened to be lean years—all excess going to the government; regular dividends and interest on bonds and other obligations may continue to be paid unless the director-general otherwise directs. A contract was agreed to between the government and the railroads in the present summer covering the details of these points.

To provide for the betterment in the railroads' operating facilities so much needed for the purposes of the war, the government established a revolving fund of $500,000,000. This fund is augmented by the earnings of the railroads in excess of the rental paid for them by the government. And in the first year of its control the government arranged to loan to the companies nearly $1,000,000,000, but a small part of which was ordered spent on new construction, while the rest was divided between new equipment and betterment of road-beds and terminals. The government simply does for the roads what was formerly done by private capital, makes them loans for which it takes their bonds and notes as security. Such an arrangement allows the government to make the improvements that are demanded by military necessity. To-day the Railroad Administration is operating 188 large railroad systems and 800 short lines, with a trackage of 260,000 miles. It was quickly confronted by the same problems with which the companies had been so long wrestling, rising costs of operations against low earnings. But it could do what the companies could not. It at once ordered an increase of 25 per cent in all freight rates, and raised passenger fares from 2½ cents to 3 cents per mile. The employees were making heavy demands on the companies, and the Railroad Wage Commission was ordered to investigate this question. In its report the director-general in August granted advances in wages aggregating more than $300,000,000, and these advances were made retroactive to the beginning of the year.

The operation of the roads has remained practically in the hands of the former operating officers. The corporate interests of the companies owning the railways are looked after by corporations' executive officers, who have no connection with the administration. They have continued in their places to guard the interests of stockholders and creditors. To secure efficiency of operation, the railroad mileage of the country has been divided into seven regional districts, each in charge of a regional director, an experienced railway executive. These districts are subdivided into smaller districts under directors. Under them Federal managers have charge of important single divisions or groups of smaller divisions. General managers direct the still smaller units. All of these directors and managers have severed their connections with the corporations, transferring their allegiance to the administration.

The effect of this unified control has been a more direct routing of traffic and a consequent saving in time and money. Under the old system there could be no competition in freight or passenger rates; but there was competition to get business by advertising and the employment of solicitors. It is estimated that by the consolidation of ticket offices and the abandoning of advertising, many millions will be saved. Inasmuch as the government receives all the money paid in, there is no object in any company carrying freight consigned to it over unnecessarily long lines. The freight can be rerouted over lines that carry it to its destination by the shortest way possible. Under the old system two companies would have competing passenger-trains leaving one point for another point at the same time. Between large centres there were many duplications of this kind which it has been possible to eliminate, with great saving of cost. The need of the roads for freight movement, as well as for the purpose of economy, has led to the cutting down of unnecessary passenger traffic as far as possible. East of the Mississippi passenger-trains that travelled more than 25,000,000 miles per year have been cut off, while west of the river there has been a saving of more than

20,000,000 miles. Other economies have been effected by providing for the common use of terminals by railways that were formerly competing. The standardization of locomotives and freight-cars, will, it is expected, make for increased efficiency and the saving of money.

While the public has suffered inconvenience by the curtailment of passenger service and has had an added drain put on its pocket by increases in rates, it has borne the change with patriotic good nature, realizing that efficiency in railroad operation was one of the factors in the winning of the war. Vast quantities of food and war materials and large numbers of troops had to be moved to the Atlantic seaboard, and this could only be done successfully with unified control. Government operation of the railroads was a war measure. Whether or not it will continue as a peace measure remains to be seen. If the roads are turned back to their owners, as it is promised they will be, some may find themselves to have suffered great hardship, while others may have benefitted greatly by the period of government financing. The "unscrambling of the eggs," will be a difficult problem.

The government had to take over the operation of the railroads as a war measure, because the unscientific treatment of them for so many years had enfeebled them for war-work. They had been heckled by politicians of all parties. They had been hampered in their growth by Federal and State commissions. Radical politicians always speak of them as though they were run for the benefit of a few stockholders and bondholders, and are, therefore, fair game for attack. As a matter of fact, the number of those who have their money directly invested in them runs into millions. More than that, fully one-half of the people of the country have an indirect financial interest in them. There are over 10,000,000 savings-banks depositors in the country, and more than 30,-000,000 industrial workers who carry insurance against death and casualty. Through these banking and insurance institutions their money has been invested in what should be a security as safe as any in the world. When the war is over these millions of investors will watch with concern the future of their properties, and it is doubtful that the majority of Americans would quietly acquiesce in the continuatica in times of peace of a policy of railroad control which would leave the finest transportation systems in the world mere shuttlecocks for the battledores of politics.   It is more probable that from the present experiment there will be worked out a system of control which will deal fairly with the public, the investors, and the employees.

This action of the government has been called socialistic.   It was, but for the time there was no other way out of a dangerous situation. The war must be won. Realizing this, Americans have faced trainless days and seatless trains with the same cheerful willingness that they have wheatless days and gasless Sundays.

CHAPTER XV

THE COLLEGE

A BOOK such as this, which seeks to describe briefly America's mobilization for war, would not be complete without consideration of the splendid part played by our universities and colleges in the great effort. It was to them that the government had to look for the large number of officers needed for the formation of our armies. Modern warfare is a technical science. The science of war in Napoleon's day, and for many years after, was largely a matter of strategy and manœuvre. The weapons used were few and comparatively simple. To-day every science is called to the aid of the armies. The knowledge of chemistry, of mechanics, of mathematics, and electricity all play a part in the construction and operation of engines of warfare. Officers who are to lead men into battle must be experts in the use of special arms and devices that were unknown but a few years ago. Not so long since artillery fired almost pointblank at its target, but to-day it fires at an unseen target miles away, and must depend for accuracy on the niceties of mathematical calculation and observation from airplanes and outlying posts. Every branch of army service requires specialists of some kind, whether on the fighting-line or far behind it. For the command of effective fighting forces trained officers are essential. Before the Great War we had only two schools, West Point and Annapolis, whose sole purpose it was to fit young men for command in event of war, and they graduated yearly but a few hundred. When we entered the conflict, one of our crying needs was for competent junior officers.

Fortunately, there had been held, in the summer of 1915 and 1916, that series of camps for voluntary training which were attended by some thousands of young men. Of these the great majority were graduates or undergraduates of our universities and colleges whose education and discipline made them readily adaptable to the requirements of military life. From the colleges, in fact, came the first effective movement for preparedness for war. Men like Eliot and Lowell of Harvard, Hadley of Yale, and Hibben of Princeton early saw the danger of war, and in their writings and speeches urged active preparation for it. Their universities went further and to practical things. They established courses of military training to fit their young men for commissions in the officers' reserve corps. Harvard and Princeton formed infantry regiments, and Yale a field-artillery battalion. Similar interest in military training began to be taken in institutions of learning all over the country. The State universities and colleges, receiving aid from the government under the land-grant act, had long had military tactics as a part of their curricula, but these courses were only rudimentary. Now they broadened their work and sought to fit their training to modern needs. The camps in the summers of 1915 and 1916, were filled with hundreds of patriotic undergraduates who gave up their vacations to prepare themselves for the day when they believed their country would need them. When the day did come many of them were ready for duty. Yale, alone, at once sent 250 men into the artillery service. Thousands of undergraduates abandoned their academic pursuits and went to the flying-fields and training-camps. Of the 40,000 men in the officers' camps of 1917, fully 85 per cent were college graduates or undergraduates. Now not a day passes but we read of the death on the field of battle of gallant young men who hardly more than a year ago were wandering care-free over some college campus. Day by day they are going overseas in an ever-increasing flow, boys hardly more than out of their teens, who seemed to have before them all that was good in life, but now stand ready to lay down their lives that their fellows may live in freedom.

At this writing it is impossible to give accurate figures as to the number of college men in war service, but statistics compiled in midsummer by the Western Reserve University indicate that they number more than 100,000. Harvard had then sent more than 8,000 graduates and undergraduates to war; the University of California 2,000 and Columbia 4,500. Yale had sent 5,800 graduates and 927 undergraduates; the Northwestern University respectively 1,071 and 370; Purdue 1,462 and 494; Johns Hopkins 500 and 235; Massachusetts Institute of Technology 1,900 and 400; Williams 752 and 192; the University of Michigan 5,000 and 2,000; Princeton 2,423 and 532; Brown 700 and 300; the University of Washington 1,587 and 1,325. In proportion to their size the smaller colleges have done as well. The record of all is one of honor.

The conduct of the war required the mobilization of the intelligence of the country, and when it accepted the German challenge, the government instinctively turned to the colleges as the source from which it could best obtain the army of men of character and education so urgently needed. In May, following the declaration of war, a conference was held in Washington between representatives of the various associations of the institutions of higher learning, the Bureau of Education and the Council of National Defense. Here plans were outlined for patriotic service. All the facilities of the colleges were placed at the government's disposal, and they arranged to organize themselves so as to be of the greatest use in the crisis. Not only did they offer the country its finest source of intelligent man-power, but their laboratories were to prove of value in research work, and their halls and dormitories useful for military schools of all kinds. While an effort has been made to halt as little as possible the progress of higher education, the demands of the war have been such as to make it imperative that the young men of the country train themselves in military science or other sciences and technical work, a knowledge of which is of so great importance in these times. To-day nearly all of our colleges are organized on a war basis.

Before April 6, 1917, there were in many of our colleges centres of pacifism and German propaganda. Those involved were either conscientious pacifists, idealistic professors who opposed war and held that the way to whip Germany was to sit placidly by and let her whip you, or they were Germans or German-trained scholars avowedly partisans of Kultur. Our neutrality made them difficult to deal with, but when we went to war they were quickly stilled or rendered harmless. How little their influence, was shown by the answer of both faculties and students to the call to arms. Hundreds of teachers left their lecture-halls to don the uniform or to take up research work for the government; thousands of students of military age and physical fitness hurried to the ranks and the training-camps of the army and navy. Seven hundred students of the University of Michigan, and 800 of Yale left their studies for the service before their school year ended. This was true everywhere. The institutions found their faculties and student bodies depleted. In the beginning of the following collegiate year, 1917–18, the enrolments of new and old students fell off startlingly. In the higher classes, senior and junior, there was an average decrease in attendance of fully 30 per cent. The attendance at Harvard, Yale, and Princeton was cut almost one-third, and a like condition existed in nearly all the other universities. For those institutions, with small endowments, which depend largely on student fees for their support, there were threatened financial difficulties, and it would have been easier for them to have closed for the period of the war. But the government's theory was that a steady supply of college-trained men was necessary to the conduct of the war, and all of them have patriotically faced their difficulties and continued their work. They have even reached out with renewed energy to induce young men to avail themselves of the educational opportunities they give. The action of the government in utilizing their facilities for military-training purposes has helped largely to relieve many of them of the financial burdens imposed on them by the war. While they have been able to continue their academic courses, in most of them training for war has become the major part of their business. Nearly all of them have established courses giving training in some phase of army or navy work. In eight technical institutions there have been founded schools where aspirants for aviation commissions receive instruction in airplane mechanics before going to the flying-fields; institutions especially equipped for the teaching of chemistry are being used for courses in chemical warfare; Yale has developed a fine artillery school. The Reserve Officers' Training Corps of Harvard, Princeton, Michigan, California, and other universities are giving the government splendid men for commissions.

But the government is looking to the colleges not only to develop officers but to train enlisted men for special duty. Their laboratories and shops have proved of great value in developing mechanics for work in the airplane and motor-transport services, in training radio operators, and in fitting men for special branches of the naval service. Four hundred of them were recently designated to give intensive courses in military work to men of the draft age. These colleges are practically army posts. Every able-bodied undergraduate is a member of the Student Army Training Corps, while thousands of graduates, and non-college men who have shown special intelligence, have in them an opportunity to prepare themselves for service. These students are fed and clothed at the government's expense and receive the pay of privates in the army.

The study of the liberal arts in our colleges has been rudely interrupted by the war. The study of science has been greatly stimulated by the need of meeting the Hun with his special weapon. The pleasant, quiet course of college life has been disjointed and turned awry for a time. The broad spaces of the football and baseball fields are crowded with figures in khaki. The lecture-halls, which once resounded with dissertations on history and psychology, are used now for the expounding of the principles of navigation and gun-fire. We seem to be devoting all our knowledge to perfecting the art of killing. It is only for a time. Our colleges will return again to those pleasant, quiet ways. Their purpose is to teach the art of living. But those whose fortune it has been to acquire knowledge in their halls saw that there could be no decent living while Germany raged through the world. Reluctantly they turned to the art of war. And they have been proving themselves gallant soldiers in a righteous cause.

CHAPTER XVI

CONCLUSION

THE writer has endeavored in this book to picture clearly and briefly the vast problem faced by America when she entered the battle for liberty, and to show how that problem has been solved. Great difficulties have been met, and they have been overcome by the united efforts of the people. To-day the greatest army that ever followed our flag is fighting in the distant fields of France, and millions more of our men stand ready to take their place on the battle-line. The mobilization of our man-power has been one of the marvels of our history. It has been accomplished with a speed and a lack of friction that a few years ago we should have thought impossible. From the North, East, South, and West, the men have poured into our armies, and those who but a year ago were working quietly on our farms and in our shops have proved themselves as brave and resourceful soldiers as ever went into battle. The mobilization of our mechanical power has not been effected so rapidly and so well. Of the two tasks, that of finding the fighting men, and that of arming them and getting them overseas, the latter has proved the more difficult. Both tasks are being accomplished. Each day that goes by and brings its long toll of those who have given their lives in our defense makes more determined the will of the people that they shall be accomplished. There is no question as to the mind of America in this war. The States that once were most blind to the peril that lay in German ambition are to-day retiring to private life the men who in Congress obstructed the efforts for our protection.

Few sane and patriotic men to-day doubt the wisdom of our government in raising its armies by imposing the obligation to fight on every man capable of bearing arms. Twenty-five million men are on the rolls; 3,000,000 are under arms; more than a million and a half are in France, and each month the numbers increase. In no other way could such results have been obtained. That they have been obtained through the operation of the selective-service law is due to the wise way in which those in charge of the working of the law have carried out its provisions. They have not used military force. They have trusted to the patriotism of American men, and the vast mass have shown that this trust was warranted. There have been slackers, of course; there have been those who dodged the registration, and those who registered but sought to avoid its obligations by specious pleas. They have earned the country's contempt. The country's pride is in those long-limbed, brown men of ours who are charging over the steel-riddled fields of France.

It is planned next spring to have 5,000,000 men at the battle-front. Germany has declared contemptuously that it cannot be done. She declared as contemptuously that we could not move a million there this year. It has been done, as she has learned at Château-Thierry and St.-Mihiel. But to move and keep 5,000,000 overseas will demand every ounce of energy in the country. Fortunately one of the most difficult of the problems involved is fast being

solved. The submarine is being beaten. **As**
we have seen, it requires five dead-weight
tons of shipping moving on the sea to keep
one soldier in France. To carry out our military programme we must have 25,000,000 dead-
weight tons available for our army by spring.
The energy of our ship-builders is solving this
problem for us. By August 30 of the present
year the world rate of building new vessels
had exceeded the rate of their destruction by
the Germans. The August production of our
shipyards was a world record, 390,980 dead-
weight tons leaving the ways. A statement
issued by the United States Shipping Board
on September 21 shows that from the beginning of the world war until September 1, 1918,
the losses of Allied and neutral shipping by
German action were 21,404,913 dead-weight
tons. In the same period the total Allied and
neutral construction was 14,247,825 dead-weight
tons. There was added to the world's tonnage
from captured enemy vessels 3,795,000 dead-
weight tons. The excess of losses over gains
in the entire period was 3,362,088 dead-weight
or (dividing by 1.6) 2,101,305 gross tons, the

terms of shipping used in the British table before given. In the thirteen months ending September 1, 1918, the American shipyards had produced 3,017,238 dead-weight tons, showing how the construction was overtaking the destruction. It was unfortunate that we had that early delay in our ship-building programme, but in organizing a gigantic business it takes time to get the right men in the right place. To-day we have them in charge of our shipping, as the record shows. The vessels are coming from the yards in ever-increasing numbers, and our navy and the navies of the Allies are holding the undersea pirates in check.

For the mobilization of our man-power we had a clean-cut law, ably executed by General Crowder, provost marshal general, with the assistance of a great number of volunteers and the general co-operation of the people. In the mobilization of our machine-power, to equip and arm these newly gathered armies, we were less fortunate. There was at first procrastination and confusion. Here, too, as in the shipping matter, it took time to get the right men in the right place. From the start the navy worked smoothly, because it had at its head, in charge of its bureaus, able professional officers. They knew what they wanted and got it. The problem of the Navy Department, as has been pointed out, was not so difficult as that of the War Department. That we did have irritating delays in the War Department is evident from the investigations of the Senate into the aircraft and ordnance programmes. These troubles had been corrected by the end of the first year and a half of war. Able men were in charge and were seeing that we got for our armies the much-needed airplanes and guns of all calibers. While it is difficult to understand the way in which these problems were handled at first, we can find cheer today in the fact that they are now being worked out.

It has been argued in some quarters that our war preparations would have proceeded more rapidly and effectively had they been in charge of a coalition cabinet. Certainly the magnitude of the crisis called for the best intelligences of the country without regard to political parties. It has been contended that a wiser direction of the great departments of the government might have been seen had those in charge of them been appointed more for their ability and experience than out of consideration for their political affiliations. On this question there are differences of opinion. But there are no differences of opinion among true Americans as to the need of pushing the war to the utmost of our power and to victory. The intelligence of the country has stood ready at the government's call. Whatever the government has asked, the people have given cheerfully.

We know that the President has promised "force—force to the utmost—force without stint or limit—the righteous and triumphant force which shall make right the law of the world and cast every selfish dominion down in the dust!"

A people that has been pouring out its blood will not rest content until the world is freed from the horror of German rule.